A Praying

Wife in

Waiting

Seeks to Heal | to Love | to Be Whole

Visionary Ebony Nicole Smith

A Praying Wife in Waiting

ISBN: 978-1-7355668-0-1 (Paperback)

Printed in the United States of America.

First printing edition 2020.

Ebony Nicole Smith Consulting, LLC - Publisher
PO BOX 67133
Rochester, NY 14617

www.ebonynicolesmith.com

Dedicated

This book is dedicated to every woman that is in need of, and seeking, healing that is long overdue.

In addition, to my oldest sister, whom I love and for whom I pray God sends a healing that only He can give.

Contents

A Praying Wife in Waiting

How to Use This Book

Dear Praying Wife,

Now that you are on this journey of healing, wholeness, and complete love and trust in God, I, Ebony Nicole Smith, want you to understand how to use this book. So, grab a notebook, you have work to do!

A Praying Wife in Waiting was supposed to be a 90-day devotional but transformed into an anthology. I thank God for the transformation while the concept of devotional remains.

Each of the chapters are to be read one day at a time. Give yourself the space to meditate on the lessons the women have gone through, experiences shared, and guidance provided. Write down your thoughts of the chapter.

Here are some questions to consider as you write down your thoughts.

> Does what you have read sound like a situation you have found yourself in at one time? If so, how?
> Can it be relatable to a family or friend?
> How did the situation turn out for you or them?
> What lessons have you learned from it?
> Without dwelling on the past for too long, think about how you felt in those moments? Do you still feel the same way?
> Be honest with yourself and God, do you need to be healed from your past traumas?
> Are you holding on with the hopes of one day changing the past, which you know you cannot?
> Is there fear attached to your feelings? If so, why?

Of course, there are more questions you will ask yourself as you read these words, meditate on the prayers, and write down the matters of your heart. The point is for you to sit with your emotions to understand where they are coming from and why. As you do, my prayer is that God will meet you where you are to heal you in the secret places that need it.

Praying Woman of God, He will speak to you through this book and guide you into all truth. Enjoy the journey.

Ebony Nicole Smith, a Praying Wife in Waiting

A Praying Wife in Waiting

Introduction

Wives in Waiting Claim Your Boaz

Martha Hope

"And God said it is not good for man to be alone I will make him a helper comparable to himself,"

Genesis 2:18

The *helper* God mentioned was an amazing, magnificent creation called woman. Adam, when referring to her said, *"She is bone of my bone and flesh of my flesh," (Genesis 2:23).* Bone is symbolic of strength, while flesh is a representation of the meat of the body. Woman was created for man, it was written in the beginning that she would complete him in mind, body, and spirit. She is not to walk behind him, nor in front of him, but beside him, while helping him to organize his thoughts, and while nurturing him as he comes to understand God's purpose for his life.

When I reflect on my own life, on the fact that I'm seventy-six, widowed and single after fifty-three years of marriage, I've come to realize that life without my husband feels somewhat awkward, different, and sometimes lonely. My husband was a special person to me. He was my best friend, my confidante, and my personal fan club/cheerleader. Did he have faults? Did I have my own? Did we have disagreements and intense arguments? You betcha! But those things didn't stop us from falling in love, from remaining in love, and from building a life together. It was God's grace, mercy, and forgiveness that kept us, and for that I am thankful.

I remember so well the first time we met, it was at a mutual friends' house. I was fourteen years old. He asked my friend Carol to ask me if he could talk to me. I said, "Absolutely not! I don't like him. I don't like nothing about him. His ears are too big, they stick out too far from his head. No! And he better not come over here either." But let me tell you how God works. About two years later, I ran into him at the fruit stand in our neighborhood. Outside fruit stands were very popular back in the day, store on the inside, fruit stands on the outside. It was then that I realized how handsome he was. His ears didn't look too bad, and he loved fruit like I did. Not only that, but he had manners, he was kind and gentle, and he was a real southern gentleman from Tuscaloosa Alabama, a country boy in the big city. Well, we dated for three years and then he asked me to marry him. Whoa! I wasn't expecting that. I knew that it would happen eventually, I just didn't know when. I'd had plans, but God's plan and purpose took the lead. I was only nineteen and he was... Well, that's a whole 'nother story. I actually never found out how old he was until he retired in 2004, mind you, we were married in 1963. His explanation for not revealing his age was that my mother and father would've probably not let him date me if they known he was 4 years older than me. Remember, this was 1960.

Wedding bells were in the air and people started talking, family and friends, people at the church, people in the neighborhood, anybody and everybody. "It won't work," they said, "they don't match, they're too different, she's a church girl, he's too worldly," you know how folks talk. But what they didn't know was that I was praying for my husband to be, and for my marriage. Some people had given our marriage two months, some said six months, while others said they gave us possibly a year if we were lucky. Because of this, I learned to keep the business of my marriage to myself and I encourage you to keep your business, your business. Do not let others tell you what to do when it comes to your relationship unless you ask them for advice, and remember, that can sometimes have negative consequences.

You should know that you are going to have some *valley* experiences on life's journey, you can't be on the mountain top all the time. The *valley* symbolizes creation and new birth dating all the way back to the beginning of time. And guess what? In the *valley,* you can find peace to grow and the strength to figure out the next step. Don't be afraid of the *valley*.

In my relationship, I learned to respect our differences, I learned to be more patient, and I learned the importance of self-care. Self-care means that any type of abuse, be it physical, mental, or emotional, and any type of disrespect cannot be tolerated. Teach your partner how to treat you, however, in order to do that, you have to first know how you want to be treated. And remember to keep God at the helm, after all, He has all of the answers.

In the pages of this book, you will find real life experiences and answers to questions you've asked yourself about being a wife. You are not alone, many of us (women) have been there in one way or another. Be it that you're single (never married), widowed, divorced, we all have a story to tell and wisdom to share.

Questions to ask yourself while you are waiting:

1. Are you ready to submit to another person (husband)?
2. Are you carrying baggage from another relationship?
3. Have you learned to seek God's guidance and instruction?
4. Are you willing to listen more and talk less?
5. Do you know what you are looking for in a husband?
6. Do you understand the power of effective communication, respect, and forgiveness?

Life's journey is full of situations, and we must learn that what we want doesn't always happen overnight.

Helpful hints:

- Be absolutely sure of what makes you happy.
- Tell God exactly what kind of husband you want. *"We have not because we ask not"* (James 4:2).
- Don't settle, God has a plan for our lives and that is that plan is that we prosper in every area of it.
- Be patient, keep praying, keep preparing yourself, and keep expecting your dream to manifest.

Claim your Boaz and wait on the Lord!

Enjoy **"A Praying Wife in Waiting"**

Story Unfold

Poetess Raquel K. Walker

S trong hands reached out only to grab a piece of
paper, but strong hands is where my mind
lands.
He was fine to me, my eyes traced him up and
down, jaw gaping open. You didn't know me, yet,
baby, in those 60 seconds I fell for you the first
chapter of our life began.
Fast forward, years flew, tempers too, two years.
Certainly, this story was thru. We searched for
clues on how to love, Deep down I didn't want to
lose you, I choose you!
Let go and fall,
let go and fall,
let go and fall,
Out of love.
We ran out of love,
let go and fall.
Let go and fall,
Let go and fall, into true knowing true no wing.

Poetry

We felt like our love had no wings, yet we needed
to fly,
you see that moment before you knew I had seen
your strong hands, I had the audacity to write
down a novel that would be our lives,
ignoring there existed a reality, the truth of who
you were,
What those strong hands knew, what that strong
mind would create,
I knew nothing of the places within me your heart
would earn. Yet my mind allowed me to write out
this script.
It seemed our love outgrew the prewritten,
this present chapter would become the second
time I fall for you a NEW you.
Finally, I knew you, void of what I created, a real
man means to me.
I realize I had to begin to know you with Real eyes
I wanted to live the rest of our years in... Real lay
eyes on me and I'll calm the stormy seas of your
minds ship,
giving each other what we deserve, seeing each
other's worth and double it.
I'm talking smooth but I know how my path of
healing ripped and shook you.
I can still hear the ringing of white gold and
diamonds falling.

Poetess Raquel K. Walker

A Praying Wife in Waiting

I didn't want marriage anymore,
Didn't know what it was for.
I aimed to barricade my soul, yet half of your heart
blocked me from slamming shut,
heart throbbing, you pleaded for better or worse,
could it get any worse, worse there would be no
divorce.
Remember how I used to measure the depth of my
worth against the number of times you said I love
you?
Remember how the sound of your tone could turn
blue skies to rain?
I never understood all that was simply a reflection
of my own pain.
My love,
it has been a long journey
back to us
the highlight is real eyes rising on me real eyes
rising on you
Never again will I write our story without you.

Praying

Wives

Successfully Single

Reintroducing Yourself to Yourself

Regine Joseph

Allow me to introduce myself. I am a thirty-six-year-old, two-time divorcee, and mother-of-four. Funny thing about it is that even with all of that going on in my life, I really do see myself as a wife. I pray that God will give me the opportunity, once again, to find the man He has for me. Better yet, I pray God allows the man to find me.

After my last divorce, I realize that I'd given so much of myself to my ex-husband that I'd lost me in the process. I was so disoriented and off track that I did not know who I was or even where I belonged. During that phase of my life, the Holy Spirit said to me one night, "Knowing who you are is a big component of knowing where you're going and who you belong with". It was at that point that I realized I had to reintroduce myself to myself in order to be an effective wife, mother, and even friend. This is where my journey begins, with me reintroducing myself to myself. Self this is Regine. Regine, allow me to introduce you to yourself.

The process I went through while on my journey was not an easy one, it included a lot of me exposing myself. It was during that exposure that the realization of my brokenness and of the repair I was much in need of came to light. Let me start from the beginning.

I was molested twice as an adolescent, which caused me to be very guarded. How can you trust anyone when the very people you love took advantage of you? Being molested caused me to feel sexualized. As a result, I had trust issues that made me very self-conscious about my outer appearance. In high school, I'd constantly hear that I was too big or that I was too small. I was too dark skinned or I wasn't light enough. My lips were huge while everything was beautiful but my face.

After high school and going into college, I became a teenage mother. I was repeatedly told that it was the biggest mistake I'd ever made. So, seeking validation from others, right after I gave birth I immediately married my child's father only to separate from him two months later. I soon found myself in another broken relationship. I became divorced from my first marriage and instantly married someone else three months later. However, I found myself going through yet another separation two years after that, a separation that ended in a very messy divorce. I knew then that I needed some kind of help and the only person I believed could truly repair me was Christ Himself.

The first step of reintroducing myself to myself was creating a vision board. You have to have a vision of where you see yourself in order to get to where you are going. When creating this vision board, it took me about fourteen days to complete it. I continuously rearranged the pictures, the wording, the timing, because even though I knew some of what I wanted, I didn't know what I truly wanted.

Have you ever become so frustrated because you can see a vision but you can't relay it in words? Well, that was me. The vision board became clear when I allowed God to maneuver my hands to place the pieces where they belonged, and to open my heart to understanding, love, and even to the exposure of the hurt. As the hurts I had experienced became more exposed and began to manifest in ways I did not like, I realized that there were certain things from my past I'd never wholeheartedly gotten over. Immediately I understood that just because I had moved past something did not mean I had healed from it.

That's when I took the time to pray and to ask God what it would take for me to get over the hurt. He told me that it would only take the words He had given me to get over those things and those words were words of affirmation. Words of affirmation are the expressing of yourself through spoken affection, praise, or appreciation. I started writing those words of affirmation on my bathroom mirror and in other places around the house.

I soon realized that I'd needed those words most when I was alone with my negative thoughts. So, I began leaving index cards and post notes in my car. On my phone, I left reminders of how great I was and how much God loved and cared for me. I did this so that I could build myself up every time I started to feel down. I did it so that I could remind myself of who I really was.

Journaling was also another outlet for the hurt I was holding on to. It was a way in which I could express myself, and it allowed me to see where I came from and all the progress I'd made in the journey toward finding myself again. Journaling also allowed me to communicate with God, because when you're so overwhelmed and can't find the right words to pray, it's easier to write them down and communicate with God that way. Not only can God hear your prayers, He can also read them and see what you truly need.

While journaling, I began to get the idea of making a pros and cons list of what I wanted to keep in my life and what I needed to change or remove for the better. I maximized the positive and removed any negative habits that were weighing me down. The list itself was easy to make because I was already walking in Christ, so I knew what I needed to keep and what needed to let go. Though it took some time, while putting the list into action, I saw such a great change in my life. Once I saw that, I just had to go back and self-reflect. While doing so, I analyzed where I now was in my life and how far I had come in such a small amount of time. It felt as though a weight had been lifted off of my shoulders. I was finally beginning to find myself and to understand who I was once again.

My confidence came back and my relationship with God was becoming stronger. Even though I was only midway through the process, the self-reflection helped me get to where I planned to be. It allowed me to realize that if I could make it as far as I had, nothing was going to stop me from getting to where I wanted to be, or better yet, where I needed to be. The self-reflection helped me see how hurt I really was, and it showed me that I needed to begin finding new ways to release that hurt. Holding on to it was only hurting me. In fact, it was keeping me from growing and from moving. It was hindering me from becoming the better version of myself, the version I knew I could be.

Not only had I been hurt, I had also been harboring anger from all of my past relationships and all of the pain from what I had endured while growing up. The awful words that others had spoken into my life stuck with me and that had caused my anger to grow and to manifest. In turn, that harboring of anger and hurt was holding me back from the growth that I needed to better myself. All of that anger didn't sit well in my spirit and even others had begun to see that I hadn't been myself.

I soon realized that I couldn't hold on to anger and expect to be happy in life. So, I took that anger and released it onto other vessels. I used a punching bag and I wrote down everything I was angry about, everything that hurt me, and all of the awful, negative things I'd heard while growing up. I released all my anger into that bag and onto that paper and I left it all there, never to pick it up again. Doing that was an effective way to release all of that hurt and pain I'd been holding on to from the past.

It is very important to have some form of release, whether it's writing down everything that hurts you and then tearing the paper up, or whether it's screaming at the top of your lungs. It doesn't matter what you do, as long as you find an effective way to get that hurt and anger out of your heart. That is what I did to become the better version of myself and I am still evolving every single day into a better version of me. Change does not happen overnight. It takes prayer and many different steps to assist you in changing for the better.

Finding yourself after you've been broken down and lost is truly rewarding. It shows you how much God cares for you and how He wants you to evolve into something much greater than what you already are. Introducing myself to myself was not an easy process, but it was something that had to be done. Learning how to be a better version of me took time and it also took opening myself up to new experiences and new ideas. My outlook on life changed after releasing the hurt and pain I was holding on to. I became much happier within myself and in my life, I was no longer left with a burden on my shoulders.

I now take other women through the process I had to endure. I understand how alone that process can make them feel, and I understand that at times they feel as if they aren't doing enough. I would never want any other women to have that same feeling I had, or to go through what I went through alone. Since my growth, not only have I begun to help other women through their process, I have also started my own organization and several different businesses. I mentor young women so that they don't have to go through or make the same mistakes I did. God truly works in such miraculous ways that I am now traveling the world and doing things I would never have imagined myself doing when I was in that mentally broken state. I also speak and uplift different types of women. When I speak at the women empowerment conferences, I see that a lot of women have been through the same thing I've been through. Some of them are still going through what I was going through, and they feel as if they don't have a way out. Is that you?

I often remind those women of who they are and of how great they are. I give them my testimony and I help them in any way I possibly can. I do this because I know that when I was going through it all by myself, I needed someone to do that for me. And for the people that were there for me, I'm very thankful for them because they helped me and uplifted me when I needed them the most. I'm now also a certified creative life strategist and a motivational speaker. You see, once you get where God intends for you to be in life and you continuously pray and grow in Him, the blessings start to manifest in ways you never thought possible.

In the Bible, God teaches us about the effectiveness of our prayers. Matthew 7:7 says, *"Ask and it will be given to you; seek and you will find;*

knock and the door will be opened to you." That scripture stuck with me through my process because I knew what I needed and wanted in life. I just had to stay consistent in my prayers for it and believe that God would guide me through my situation.

The journey and the process I went through were very trying, but God truly does give His hardest battles to his toughest soldiers. I now realize that I went through what I did so that I could help others overcome what I once had to endure. I know myself better than I did before, and I have unwavering confidence in myself and in everything I do from here on out. I have opened my heart to love and have become at peace with every situation I went through in the past. Several people thought the position I was in was going to break me, but God allowed me to overcome it. Not only that, but I became better in the end due to the situation.

When was the last time you introduced yourself to yourself? And ask yourself if it was effective. If you haven't already done so, now is the time to introduce yourself to yourself in a life changing way.

Handling Mental Health Issues in Singleness

Berlinda Grant

The wife in waiting kneels to pray,

"Dear Heavenly Father, I thank you for your mercy and grace, dear God. God, I ask that you bless me with a husband, someone I can grow old with. God, I want to have companionship, someone I can love and that loves me back. I thank you, God, in advance, amen!"

Or maybe this sounds familiar,

"Father God, please send my husband in my direction. Send me the following:

1. A man with good credit.
2. A man with a great job.

3. A man that is tall, dark, and handsome.
4. A man with no baby mama drama.
5. A man that knows how to lead.
6. A man that has his affairs in order.

In Jesus name, amen!"

Or how about this one,

"Lord God, I come humbly to you asking that you would bless me with a husband. God, send me a man of God. A man that knows who he is, that has his affairs in order, a man that is emotionally, physically, and financially ready for a wife. I need him to want a wife and not a mother. Send me a man that is ready and that has space in his life for a Queen, a man that is fit to rule with no hang ups or baggage from his past. Amen!"

Well, wife in waiting, our prayers to God put us on the right track, mainly because those prayers demonstrate that we acknowledge our need to put, and go to, God first. After all, He is the one that can do all things! The only problem is that we tend to list what *we want* in a mate. Although there is nothing wrong with that, we have the tendency to forget to ask God to reveal to us who and what we *need*. In addition to telling God what we want and need, we also forget to ask Him to help us work on ourselves so that we are prepared for the man we are asking Him for.

In our prayers and preparation for a husband, the most important thing we need to do is ensure that we are also addressing our own health and wellness. What better time to do that than when we are in our singleness? It does not matter how you arrived at your single state, be it you are a young adult and single, divorced and now single, or widowed and now single, we must embrace our singleness. And the first step in this embracing process is ensuring your wellness.

There are eight dimensions of wellness: emotional, environmental, financial, intellectual, occupational, physical, spiritual and social. Let us zero in and focus on mental/emotional wellness.

Your mental wellness pertains to how you handle or deal with difficult and adverse life situations. In addition, your mental health directly affects how you respond to, and how you express yourself in relationships. Now, hear me correctly, all areas of wellness need to be maintained in your life, but managing your mental issues is a very critical component of that health management. So, before you get engulfed into a relationship, let's identify and handle your mental health issues.

Mental health issues are an exhaustive list, but some common matters are anxiety, schizophrenia, PTSD (post-traumatic stress disorder), bi-polar depression, and clinical depression. These disorders, along with others, can make it extremely difficult to obtain and sustain a healthy relationship. The reason is because they involve how you think, how you feel, how level your mood is, and how appropriate your behavior is. In a nutshell, your daily life functioning is affected.

My big battle was with clinical depression. According to the American Psychiatric Association (2020), depression is a common and serious medical illness that negatively affects how you feel, the way you think, and how you act. I went years without understanding that I was battling depression. Depression made it difficult for me to develop as a teenager, difficult for me to parent my children as a young adult, and difficult for me to identify and navigate toxic relationships in my adulthood.

In my later childhood and early teens, I began to experience physical abuse at a high level with a family member. This experience lasted for years, until I moved away at seventeen. However, in conjunction with the physical abuse I experienced, my ultimate experience was with sexual assault. The assault occurred during my mid-teen years, and it was at gunpoint with the barrel of that gun aimed at my temple. This attack was not committed by a family member, but by a member of the community that I knew of but did not know personally.

After I had been sexually assaulted, I did what many women do most of the time, I said nothing. That experience not only compounded what I was already dealing with, it also put me in a headspace where I did not have the capacity to process or cope with what had occurred. And because I chose to keep quiet about the event, that meant there would be no therapy or help to heal mentally and to recover from the experience.

Now, what I did not know was that just because I kept what happened to myself and attempted to live what I considered normal life, didn't mean I was ok. Even though that event was the staple of my depression, it went unaddressed well into my very late 30's, causing a cycling of moods from time to time.

By this time in my life, I was a mentally exhausted parent, trying to figure out how to function effectively. I was experiencing divorce again, repeating my pattern of entering and ending toxic relationships that also included physical abuse. I was at a place where I couldn't possibly make wise decisions when it came to healthy relationships because I wasn't aware of what a healthy relationship looked like. In addition, I'd had yet to take a moment in over twenty-five years to deal with my traumatic experiences.

The turning point for me was when I ended up one step away from a complete breakdown. I'd had full episodes of clinical depression and was struggling with the basic activities of daily life. I'd experienced unexplained physical ailments, homicidal thoughts (yes, I wanted to take a few people out), and fear and anger, all of which were accompanied by extended periods of sadness and extreme irritation. A return to a normal state of mind, emotionally or mentally, was essential, but it just didn't seem possible. Let's face it, there was no feeling of a promising quality of life at all and I needed to make a decision that would lead me toward restoration. I needed to deal with my issues.

If you take the time to work through your mental issues, you will be able to effectively communicate, you will learn to trust again, and for some of us, we will be able to trust for the first time. But first, you must work through your anger, your hate, or your fits of rage, all which can be by products of mental issues that have yet to be resolved. The last thing you want is to be a praying wife in waiting, expecting a husband that has it all together while all you have to present is pieces of a wife. Handling your issues while you are single gives your relationship a strong enough foundation upon which to build a lasting bond. By working on this aspect of your mental health, you will be in a space where you can trust, and where you can commit to the development, the phases, and the lifespan of a marriage, all because you're able to process and recognize those things within yourself.

So, praying wives in waiting, let's master the handling of your mental health issues. The first thing I would suggest you do while you are single is identify where you are mentally, and what mental issues you are battling. Mental health issues can paralyze you emotionally and make it exceedingly difficult to be in a meaningful relationship. Mental health issues will not just affect your intimate relationships, it will also affect the relationships within your family circle, your work relationships, your business relations, etc.

Your awareness of your issues is the first step toward handling those issues. Therefore, once you have established where you are mentally, accept it! Internally, you have to give yourself permission to feel how you feel. Be true to you. By being aware of where you are mentally, accepting where you are, and then making steps toward change, you will begin to build a confidence in your ability to overcome that is beyond measure, trust me. You won't be prideful or boastful, you'll be confident that what you may be facing isn't the end product, but instead the making of a great product. You can do some great things when you are true to you. Plus, being true to self-demands that others handle you with respect. In addition, you will decrease the risk of any old Joe Blow sliding into your life with nonsense, taking you off course, or filling the space of the one who actually should be taking a spot in your life.

There are men out there that don't have the best intentions, men that have a knack for sniffing out wounded women. Those same men will take you on a tailspin journey that can last for years, sometimes decades, until your confidence is depleted. When you accept where you are, you can move forward and start addressing those things you need to deal with. Once you do that, the fact that you have the issues won't keep you hiding and pretending to be something or someone other than who you really are. Your decision to deal with mental issues in your life will create a level of boldness in you.

Getting to the root of the problem requires the seeking of help from health professionals and practitioners. This step can be a challenge because it requires you to talk to someone you don't know about your issues, about the deep, the dark, and the ugly things you would rather keep to yourself. Seeking professional help has more than one level to it. You may not only be required to speak to a professional about where the issue stems, you also may need medications for a period as well. During counseling, the root of some things you've been dealing with may be easily apparent, but there are also some things that have been buried so deeply that you don't even know they're there. Those things may not be so readily apparent.

At times, and according to severity, in-patient treatment may be necessary. That's why a professional is essential in getting to the root cause of your mental concerns. However, having a circle of other trustworthy people that you can talk to during your process will assist in your treatment. Socially connecting to others is often a great supplement.

Treatment for mental issues isn't like a five-day course of antibiotics, it takes time. So be patient with yourself. It is important to stick to treatment plans and to be consistent with counseling and with doing the work that leads to a better you. Don't let guilt, shame, or the stigma of needing professional help take your focus away from your healing. On any journey you have to put one foot in front of the other in order to get to your desired location. While on this journey, be aware of triggers and of how to maneuver over, under, or around them so that you can stay your course.

Lastly, remember that adverse events in our lives can be tender and sensitive areas, so continue to guard those areas after treatment. Do self-checks to maintain your progress and remember that you don't have to be a superhero after treatment.

Always check yourself to make sure you don't regress.

After doing everything to ensure your own mental and emotional health, when God answers your prayer and sends you "the one" you'll have great confidence. You'll have a version of self-love that is remarkable, and you'll have the capacity to love without limits. You'll also have coping strategies in place to help you rise above if you're having some not so great moments. And finally, you will be able to navigate positively through, and respond effectively, to the hurdles and hazards that come with being in a relationship.

Let's recap:

5 Tips to Mastering Mental Health Issues
1. Know where you stand.
2. Accept and be true to what you are experiencing.
3. Seek help to get to the root cause of what you are experiencing.
4. Follow treatment plans, establish how to identify and to cope with your triggers.
5. Self-checks to sustain your progress and recovery

Be truthful, if God sent someone your way right now, are you in a space where you can give one hundred percent of yourself while exploring a relationship? Or will you be so weighed down with your baggage that you are unable to be in a mentally stable place? If you are not in a mentally healthy place, I urge you reach out and make the necessary steps to be in position for the husband God is preparing for you!

Wives in waiting, love yourself enough to keep your health and wellness a priority. I strongly believe that you can't do this without God. He is the one that is preparing that husband you're earnestly praying for. While He is preparing him to be that husband, He needs your cooperation as He prepares you to be a wife. Direct your prayers to God first. Ask Him to reveal your mental issues, to help you with your mental issues, and to assist you with getting to the root of the problem. Ask God for guidance and direction on accessing the right professional, one that can help you while God works within you for healing and restoration. Remember, we can do all things through Christ, this is proven to be true.

Wives in waiting and current wives, I'm believing with you that you will put the handling of your mental issues on the top of your list and I celebrate with you in advance!

If you would like to take a step into wellness, reach out to us for a wellness assessment at www.berlindagrant.com.

References: (www.psychiatry.org, 2020)
www.psychiatry.org. retrieved June 2020

Single Season Harvest

Poetess Kalina Harrison

My single season is not always storms of loneliness
Nor is it constant sunshine in solitude.
It's more like sweeping winds of the attitude of gratitude.
I am learning to have faith in God's provisions,
Exchanging my cloudy view for His perfect vision.
I am now including Him in all of my decisions.
Sometimes I don't understand,
Sometimes I feel forgotten.
Thankfully, feelings are fleeting, and God's Word is permanent. How can I be so short-sighted?
How can I forget all of those out of the blue miracles?
If He remembers to make the sunshine and the flowers bloom,

Surely, He has a plan for me to meet my groom!
No longer will I disappoint God with doubt,
"For I consider that the sufferings of this present are NOT worth comparing with the glory that is to be revealed to us." Romans 8:18
Nothing supersedes God's Promise!
In fact, the Promise is on the way,
It will not fail or delay.
I am committed to fully honoring God and maximizing my faith.
I deserve the richness of God's gifts,
But first, I must submit.
My will, plans, and goals must all be given to the Most High,
He calls me daughter and bride.
He has a monsoon of blessings during every season of my life!
The only time I will fight is when I am fighting my flesh,
The Spirit will sustain me, and there's no need to second guess.
NO matter the season, God sends a downpour of abundance!

Why Do I Fail at Relationships?

Ebony Nicole Smith

*R*elationships... How many of us have failed at them? *Relationships...* How many of us want to forget them? *Relationships...* How many of us want to go back in time and ignore the, *"Hello, my name is John Doe. What's yours?"* *Relationships...* How many of us have asked ourselves, "Why do I fail at relationships?"

It's funny to me how words spoken out of what seems to be love can be painted with deceit. I believed the words of a man that were spoken in such colorful ways, words that were used to paint a picture of hope, of a future, and of assurance. However, his words would never become the vision

I thought we both desired them be. After that last "situation-ship" I was in, I made up my mind to find the answer to *why I fail at relationships*. However, instead of finding that answer, many more questions arose. Questions like, *why am I never good enough? Why can't men be faithful to me? Am I too fat, too dark skinned, not tall enough, not pretty enough?* The questions of self-doubt and insecurities within myself came one right after another, leading me down a rabbit hole of both sadness and depression.

The more I thought about why I kept failing at what I desired the most, the heavier my heart had become. Bitterness crept in, unpacked its baggage, and made itself at home. As I searched for the answer, I struggled to find fault in me, of course. The issues were entirely their fault as to why we didn't work out. They were the culprits, not me. So, I told myself that I would never hurt again and that the *Ebony Bank of Love* had enough for one more withdrawal. After that, it would be shut down for life! NO EXCEPTION.

Loaded Question

I remember feeling alone on my journey toward finding the answer to my question. This loneliness was because I wasn't in a place, mentally or emotionally, to discuss it with any of my close friends, because I lacked the words to explain it, and because I didn't want them to think I was weak. Not that they would ever think of me that way, however, I felt a lot of pity on myself and thoughts of being judged was one of the effects of it.

I hadn't gotten far into my journey before I heard a small, still voice say, "I Am your Father. Let Me be who I Am." It may seem random and unrelated to the question around my relationships with men, but this statement from God is definitely related. Why? Because all the while I was looking for the answers, I'd forgotten the one question that would change my life and perspective: *Why doesn't my dad want me?*

That's a loaded question, right? And as an adult, I would never think to ask that loaded question of myself or think that anyone else would to ask it either. However, the truth is that the answer to that question is none of my business. See, when I decided that my biological father's actions toward me were no longer my business, I was left with a void that my Heavenly Father stepped in to fill.

The decision to no longer seek my natural father came to be when I noticed that he treated me like the men I had previously dated. Different men, same characteristics. Broken promises, only calling when he needed something, hardly being available to and for me, all of those were common threads in each of my relationships with men. In essence, I had been dating my father. It still amazes me today how I even functioned in such unhealthy, one-sided relationships, but through it all, I kept giving it everything that made me *me*, while receiving the absolute minimum from them.

The moment I allowed God to step into the place of my Father was the moment He became everything this *little girl* ever needed, wanted, and desired. I found myself no longer wanting my dad, but wanting my DAD. Here's the difference between my father and my Father: the lessons taught to me by both of them. The lessons taught by my father would be the very lessons I would endure repeatedly. Some women want to date a man like their father, not me! I somehow managed to attract the very man I didn't want. The liar, the empty promise-giver, the undecided one. What was it in me that was so strong that it caused those men to come for me? Alternatively, was it that I was searching for my father, for the man I wanted my father to be, in them?

The relationship with my father was so damaging to me, that I had to learn to trust my Father and believe Him to be different than my father. I didn't understand how much hurt I had carried in my heart for so long in regard to the image of a father-figure. Because I had been so hurt and for so long, even with God, I didn't immediately accept Him as the father figure I needed and wanted. He had to gain my trust and I had to allow Him the opportunity to do so. People would easily say, "Trust God," but if you have trust issues, even God has to work for your trust.

My Father never let up on gaining my trust, however. He showed me how to trust Him by revealing to me the call on my life. With that, He would tell me personal information about someone that would blow my mind, and then He would have me tell the person what He said. At first, I was very much afraid. It would take me a lot of back and forth with Him before I would move as He instructed me. He would give me details about something someone was praying for, then He would have me reveal the answer to them. It was in these precious and somewhat testy moments that I learned to trust Him, but there was still more work to get me to fully do so.

As time went on, God kept talking, kept ministering to me, and I kept inching toward the level of complete trust in my Father. For me, however, I had some serious trust issues that stemmed from childhood concerning male figures, and those issues didn't stop just because the One trying to convince me to trust Him this time was God. Nope, they remained firmly in place, but He patiently proceeded to show me why and how to trust Him. It wasn't an easy road to travel, I had to let go of everything I knew a father to be and allow Him to be the ultimate example I deserved.

I share this because the root of my trust issues was planted *loooonng* before I knew God. However, He knew me. He was well aware that I would have trouble believing He would do what He said. After years of being let down, I had to finally put my trust in the One that could do all things but fail.

How to Trust God:

1. **Read His Word**. I dove deep into Abraham to help me build my trust in God. I choose to study one of the most faithful men in the bible, besides Jesus, because His faith didn't waver despite what God had said compared to what He had told Him to do (Gen. 22:1-14).

2. **Determine the Root of Your Trust Issues**. Here is where you must be really honest for you to get to the root cause of your trust issues. Sit with your emotion and allow *it* to tell you the truth you've hidden deep in your heart. This might be painful, but in the end, it will be well worth it.

3. **Give Him a Chance to Prove Himself Worthy of Your Trust**. Just as you would allow a man to gain your trust, a man that can fail you, give God that same courtesy. Just ask Him to show you how to trust the Truth instead of the lie you've been accustomed to for so long.

Write About Your Husband

In 2017 God said, *"Write down fifty things you NEED in a husband."* What? I knew I had to be tripping. I was totally against writing a list because at that point I wanted what God wanted me to have. However, following my moment of rebellion, God was so kind as to add, "*I know what you NEED. I want you to tell me what you NEED.*" At first, I didn't get why I needed to tell my Father what I needed when He already knew what I needed, but later I would come to understand. In response to His command, I prayed, "*Lord, I am going to do what You said. I ask that You join me, help me write this list.*" And He did. Today, I have sixty things, points, elements, must-haves for my husband on my list. There were moments that I had to ask for help because I had become stuck in identifying what I wanted. At those times He would so sweetly tell me what to add. He blew my mind over and over during the writing of my husband. I'll share with you some of my list.

My top six needs and desires:
1) Loves God.
2) Has a relationship with Jesus.
3) Can hear from the Holy Spirit.
4) A great communicator.
5) A man after God's heart, a protector of my heart, and knows his own heart.

6) One to whom I don't have to prove that I am worthy of respect and a great love.

I want to challenge you, like God did me, to write a list of fifty things you desire and need in a husband. Now, when you are thinking of your needs, I want you to say them aloud. Example, "I need him to..." or whatever you can think of to say out loud. Here's the point, God is interested in what we want, not what we don't want (Mat. 7:7). If we ask Him for a particular type of man, I am believing for you and for me that He'll create that man just for us. From this point on, be mindful of how you speak about your husband, God is listening and so is the enemy!

What I learned about the list is that it wasn't only for God to know, but for me to know as well. If I know what I need, I'm able to reject when a man is giving me something that isn't what I have asked God for. Looking at my top six needs and desires, I can immediately recognize that if he lacks those things, I don't have to waste my time with him. And I truly feel okay with this. I am asking for one-of-a-kind man. Only one will be able to wear the coat of favor God has waiting for him, a coat he'll receive when he makes me his wife (Proverbs 18:22).

My hope for you, my dear sister in Christ, is that you become healed, whole, trusting of God, and that you will tell Him what *YOU NEED*. Even if you're not interested in becoming a wife, healing is the children's bread, darling. Get what you deserve (Mat 15:22-29). There is a reason why I failed at relationships and there's a reason for you too. If you are really ready to know the reason for the failure, just ask Him. He's waiting to answer you and to show you how to become a successfully single woman of God.

I want you to download my free affirmations e-book for praying wives, waiting and married, from my website ebonynicolesmith.com. It will give you prayers and scriptures that can help you in both your single and your married season.

Prayer:
Father, forgive me for my complaint against the *waiting* I am in. I know I am *waiting*, not in vain, but in You. I am *waiting* on Your love that is incomparable. I am *waiting* on Your grace. I am *waiting* as I am being sharpened and transformed

into the woman You created me to be. However, while I am waiting, I become saddened when I see that others have what I desire. I know this is my journey and that there will be no one to travel it beside me (Heb 12:1-2), but Father, I ask that You Help me with being okay with this *wait*. I know I must wait, and I will, but I don't want to be like the children of Israel who wanted a king because everyone else had one. You gave them what they wanted when all they needed was You (1 Sam. 8:1-22). I just want You, plus other things. Help me to be okay with not having the other things right now. Help me. I'm alone, but I'm not lonely. I can call someone to fill that void, but I don't want just anybody because I'm not just any woman.

Thank You for hearing me and for giving me the strength for this important season of *waiting*. Thank You for not giving me what I want just because it's what others have. Thank You for keeping me covered and closed off so that not just any man will see and find me. Thank You for answering my request. I count it done and to be seen when you deem it and me ready.

I love You from now until my very last breath. Amen.

Out of Order

A.B. Brumfield

Let all things be done decently and in order.

1st Corinthians 14:40

To be a single Christian woman, a wife in waiting, was at first a very difficult thing for me. I hated it, I hated it, I absolutely hated everything about it. Why? Because first, I didn't understand how I was even single to begin with. Second, I was a hopeless romantic who just loved being in a relationship. And third, because one of my greatest fears was of growing old alone.

Now, when I say that I didn't understand how I was even single to begin with, I mean that I was genuinely confused about how I *could* be single and I was sincerely struggling to understand how I even got to that single place. You see, I thought that I was the girlfriend that everyone would want. Not because I thought I possessed the body and the beauty that surpassed every woman in existence, that was never my mindset. No, I thought I was the kind of woman that men would want because I was the long-term relationship woman, the woman that knew how to stick it out and stick with my man through the good times and the bad. I was always in it for the long haul and my relationships were serious, very serious, and they each lasted for no less four years.

In these relationships, I was the girlfriend that was faithful, the girlfriend that wanted more from a man than his money. I was the girlfriend that would do everything I could to elevate my man so that no matter how good he was when we first became a couple, he would still be in a better place if he and I were ever not a couple. I knew how to, and did, let the man lead. I knew how to, and did, prioritize him and lift him up with my words and with my actions. And I knew how to be, and was, a help meet to him in every sense that I knew to be (Genesis 2:18 KJV), even though he wasn't yet my husband. However, even with me knowing and doing all of that, I still found myself outside of a relationship and completely single.

And I hated it!

During this single season, I would often wonder why God would allow everyone else to experience love and marriage while He had me on the sidelines in a bubble of invisibility that made it impossible for men to see me. It drove me insane as I tried to understand why God would bless people that I knew weren't being as faithful, as dedicated, and as loving a wife as I would be in a relationship. I lacked understanding as to why He would allow people that were serial cheaters to have mates that were loyal and faithful while I, someone that was loyal and faithful, had no one. And I just could not grasp why a child of God would not be blessed with the gift of marriage while those that didn't even have a relationship with God, that didn't even claim God, could be, and *was,* blessed with it.

I was confused.
I was angry.
I was dead wrong!

You see, although I knew that what I had to offer a man was priceless, what I had to offer God was not. Up to that point, what I had to give God was conditional and finite. It was conditional in that I would give God only what I could and only under the conditions that it didn't cause too much discomfort and it didn't get in the way of something I really wanted. And what I had to offer God was finite in that I had limits to what I was willing to give Him. If I had to sacrifice too much, or if I had to choose between making Him, God, happy, or making the man happy, I would choose to please the man and expect God to understand.

In that season of my life I knew *of* God, I didn't really *know* Him. I had no real relationship with Him, wasn't looking for a relationship with Him. In fact, I didn't even know that I *should be* having a relationship with Him, or *how I should treat Him* if I *did* have a relationship with Him. I knew almost nothing about God except that I could hear Him when He spoke to me and I harbored the false belief that He was there to answer my prayers, to give me what I wanted. Beyond that, I didn't give Him much consideration at all.

I expected God to be my genie in a bottle. Every time I went to Him, I fully expected Him to make my every wish come true. I wanted Him to provide me with whatever I requested while I gave Him almost nothing. To be completely honest, the only thing that I would give God was the acknowledgement that He was my Savior whenever, and *if ever*, the conversation came up. Don't get me wrong, I would tell people about Him, would do what I knew to do to lead people to Christ, but when it came to having a relationship with God, when it came to having real fellowship with God, I didn't. I didn't even bother to.

I put all of my focus on what I really wanted. A man, a relationship. There was one man in particular that I catered to, spoiled, and made some real hardcore sacrifices for. I did the most for my man while doing the minimum for my God. God was barely, and I do mean *barely*, on my mind. But my man? He was always on my mind, always my focus, always on the forefront of my everything. At that time in my life, I thought I had God, I thought I knew all there was to know about God, so there was no reason for me to put any effort into Him. And to a certain degree, I took God for granted because I knew God would never leave me. However, if I made that man uncomfortable, that man probably would leave me, and I just couldn't have that!

In truth, I had chosen that man over God. In even more truth, that man had even more value to me than God. I had made my man my God! And being the loving God that He is, He humbly took a step back and let me see just how having a man as my God would play out.

It.
Almost.
Destroyed.
Me!

In more ways than I can even begin to count.

But God!

You see, the God that I served, contrary to what I thought, was always there. He was always in the midst of that relationship, always protecting me, always pulling me to Him even though I was as of yet unaware of what He was doing. He was honoring His Word to never leave me while I was busy putting Him on the back burner and may have left Him if that man had asked me to. He was honoring my free will to be with that man even while that man was dragging me through every ring of hell! But what I didn't know, what I wouldn't find out until much later, was that God always had it all under control. He knew that the man was the person that would bring me closer to Him. And He knew that the hell that man would put me through was what it would take for me to start calling on Him.

And.
I.
Did!

What I didn't see then, but what I clearly see now, was that as I was being abused in that relationship in every way except physical, I was constantly crying out to God, constantly moving closer to God, constantly developing communication with God. I would pray, fast, pray more. I would ask God questions, beg God to help me, then wait for His response. I began to study Him, learned to trust Him, kept seeking Him, trusting His counsel. By the time that relationship was over, *completely over*, and I had entered my single season, I was absolutely in love with God in a way that I had never been in love with that man! I'd made it through the storm and had reached the other side.

I was now saved, sanctified, and single.

And very confused!

I was truly baffled as to how I could be so good to someone and still find myself alone. However, it was in this confusion that God began to show me why He'd allowed me to go through that storm, and why He was now allowing me to be alone. That revelation process was very humbling.

It shamed me when God made me look back and see just how desperately I'd wanted that man more than I'd wanted Him. I was more focused on that man than I'd been focused on Him. I loved that man more than Id' loved Him. And why should God allow me to be that good to a man while not sharing any of that goodness with Him, my Creator, my Savior, my God?

He's a jealous God (Exodus 34:14 KJV).
Therefore, He wouldn't allow it!
Then, God went deeper!

My loving Father showed me that in my frantic quest to be a wife, I wasn't operating from a place of Godly love, I was operating from a place of fear. Fear of not having a husband love me because I didn't, and didn't *know how to*, love myself. And since God does not give us a spirit of fear (2nd Timothy 1:7 KJV), the first thing He had to do was let me be alone so that I could face and conquer that fear. Then, He had to teach me what being a Godly wife was really all about.

My goal had been to love a man so much that I would never run the risk of being alone and being without love. If I could just get him to see how wonderful *I* was, then he would love me and marry me, and we would live happily ever after. Without even realizing it, my goal had been to focus on my husband and to get my husband to focus on me. By doing that, I was taking the focus off of God! And God would not allow that to be so. That wasn't the kind of Christian or the kind of wife He wanted me to be.

God had it in mind for me to do things decently and in order. To desire and love anything more than I loved God was nowhere near decent and not even remotely close to being in order. So, I needed to be stilled, I needed to be alone, I needed to spend time in seclusion and in isolation with my Father. And if I could do that, if I could be faithful to God, loyal to God, obedient to God, then God would prepare and *repair me* so that I could be a good wife to my husband.

So, after understanding that I'd been out of order, I humbly allowed God to get me in order. I studied the bible every morning and every night. I sought His wisdom and a deep understanding of Him and His word. I praised God, sometimes with tears rolling down my face. I gained a deep understanding of everything He had done for me and had been to me over the years, especially when I deserved nothing from Him. And I talked to God all of the time about every detail of my life, about the good, the bad, the downright sinful. I let Him into every aspect of me. It took some time developing that profoundly personal relationship with God, but when I had done so, I recognized that I was even more in love with Him. I understood that no other person or thing in existence could get me to love them like I loved God.

Now, I no longer hate my single season, I've embraced it. I spend this time with God loving Him with all of my heart. Not because I expect anything in return from my Father, but because I genuinely want to love God whether I ever have a husband or not.

I communicate with God daily. Because I'm doing that, God is perfecting my communication skills so that I'll know how to effectively communicate with my husband. I study God daily, and in the process, He's teaching me how to study my husband so that I can know how to please him. I spend time becoming a better Christian, as a result, God is teaching me how to be the best wife. And most importantly, I spend time making God the center of my life so that my husband can see that and know to do the same. And while giving the entirety of my heart to my Father, God is teaching me how to properly give my heart to my husband.
I am, in all aspects of my life, by constant communion with God, learning to put and keep God first. And by doing so, I will never make the mistake of making my husband my god.

I will never put him before God. I will never teach or allow him to put me before God. I will never have a marriage and a love that is so out of order that God comes in last place in that marriage if He comes in at all. I will be the Proverbs 31 wife. Not because I taught myself to be so, but because God set me apart, kept me alone, and took the time to teach me to be so.

God taught me how to love Him.
He taught me how to love myself.
And He taught me how to love my husband.
It is for that reason that my marriage, my threefold cord, will not be easily broken.
I am no longer out of order!

Heavenly Father,
It is my most sincere desire that every woman reading this will **seek You, study You,** and **always keep You first**! I pray that we **never put the creation before the Creator** (Romans 1:25). And I pray that we **never love anyone, or anything more than we love You**. (Matthew 22:37 KJV)
In Jesus' name,
Amen!

The Coming Out of the State of Addiction

Tonika Goode

Webster defines addiction as the fact of or the condition of being *addicted* to a particular substance, thing, and or activity. To be *addicted* is defined as being physically and mentally dependent on a particular substance or thing and being unable to stop taking it, or to stop doing it without incurring adverse effects.

Every activity we see or engage in has a root cause. With addiction, the root cause is *rejection* or *abandonment*. The definition of rejection is the dismissing of or the refusing of a proposal, an idea, etc. It is the spurning of a person's affection.

Abandonment is defined as the action or fact of abandoning or being abandoned; rejected.

When this topic was presented to me, or should I say when the question of a topic was asked of me, what immediately dropped into my spirit was that I was always looking for projects to fix. Now, when I say fix, I don't mean manage as in when a woman is given some thing or some situation to manage, to bring in order, or to align. I mean fix the way some men have the innate ability to fix things. However, as single women waiting for marriage, we should come to understand that our job is to manage whatever is given to us. In this chapter, I will gracefully attempt to make sense of what I'm saying to you about this *addiction*. Then we will uncover the root of a thing and learn why uncovering the root of a thing is important. My root was abandonment and rejection and I'm going to take this opportunity to teach a little bit on those topics.

In order to fix anything, you have to first find out the root cause of it. If you don't know the root cause of it, you will simply be displaying to yourself and to everyone around you, symptoms of a thing you don't understand. My root was rejection and abandonment, which showed up in the form of addiction.

I used to be the type of person that picked what we will call "projects" in my dating season. "Projects" were men that needed to be fixed. In other words, they did not have all of the essentials to take care of themselves, let alone the essentials to take care of me and a family. Multiple times in my life, I chose to, or felt that I needed to, be with someone that needed to be fixed. Maybe he'd have a job, but that was about it. He wouldn't have a place of his own and he'd usually have to borrow someone else's car to get around. The men I would choose couldn't even pay bills or manage a check book or pay a utility bill, and if they did manage to have a car, they couldn't pay car insurance.

Now, at those times in my life I had the mindset that their lack of ability to handle those things was okay because I could do it. Heck, I *was* doing it and had *been* doing it since I was sixteen years old. I would look at the situation and tell myself that at least he was going to work and was trying. The women in my family were very domineering and if the man didn't or couldn't do something, they would and always did. Growing up exposed to that, was how I was able to take on so many projects without having an issue with doing so. Now some would ask, "What's wrong with that?" Well, if we're kingdom minded women and want our boys to grow up to be kings, we have to teach them that they have to be men that go out and work.

2nd Thessalonians 3:10 declares that, "If a man does not choose to work, neither shall he eat". The man is supposed to be the provider, to give security, and to establish structure. However, we have been taught in society that if we, the women, are doing those things, it's perfectly ok. We've been led to believe that the man doesn't have to do those things and thus he is not responsible for those things. To add to what society has taught us, experience has taught us that when a woman expects a man to step up and be the provider, to offer the security, and to establish the structure, the man will cower down. It is likely that he will become intimidated and call us out of our name. What we must come to realize is that we don't have to accept that and that if we want better, we must be willing to wait.

Now, waiting is not always a bad thing. It gives us time to find our worth. To explain this in greater detail, let me give some backdrop. You see, when we recognize what we are addicted to, and what the root of our addiction is, only then can we begin to make the corrections needed to heal ourselves from whatever our issues may be while we are waiting to become that virtuous wife. In order to be a virtuous wife we have to have the qualities of a virtuous wife. This means that we have to know the difference between managing and fixing. We have to understand that our kings should have the same things that we have in order to lead us. In other words, he should have a house, a car, a job, or a career. Only then can we come together and boss up together. Once he has established these things, we can complete our team and not spend time in our relationship competing for a position. However, sometimes we may have to wait on this kind of relationship.

Being afraid of waiting brings about the issue of settling. Some women settle for relationships they don't want to be in because they believe that if they leave it will take forever for them to find another relationship. So, they'll settle for things they don't really want, things they'll be triggered to fix, just so they don't have to be alone. But why settle and spend your time trying to fix everything when waiting on God will get you Gods best and will allow you to present your best to your mate? It is better to wait and allow God to work on you until He sends you His best than it is to accept whatever show's up and have to deal with the consequences of that.

What I'm saying is that once you realize you have an addiction, you have to find out what your triggers are so that you can properly deal with them and move forward accordingly. This may not happen overnight. Queens, when you take the time to realize your addictions and to learn your triggers, it opens up a whole other level of intimacy between you and God and it allows your healing to begin. You will or can be working on yourself, look up and your King is standing in front of you complementing you on the DIAMOND that you have become.

Queens, know this one thing, when I learned that I had an addiction and sought God on how to deal with it, I was able to see things much clearer. I could see the counterfeit men, or counterfeit diamonds, coming at me from a mile away. I could dismiss them without an attitude and not waste their time or more importantly, my own time. Let's be honest here and understand that time is something we can't get back and I want to spend my time learning to be wiser and smarter. I don't want to spend my time working harder and becoming bitter. While acknowledging the fact that I had an addiction, I was then able to identify that addiction and pluck it up from the root. Because I did that, we all win. My children win, my king wins, and the kingdom wins!

There are more DIAMONDS in the world than there are under coal.

And just remember this: iron sharpens iron and only a diamond can cut another. Let's build each other up and not tear one another down. If you see my crown tilted, help straighten it, don't knock it off.

I truly hope this blessed you as much as it blessed me.

Healthy Endings

Felicia Barnett

Once upon a time, I was a young wife that lived in a very unhappy marriage. I'd met my husband in 1979 when we were both in sixth grade. However, it would be years later that we would actually reconnect and marry.

In 1986, I endured a life changing event that would alter the course of my entire life. I was in a car accident and nearly died. The following year, 1987, I married the boy I'd met in sixth grade. At this point, we were young adults, so we made the decision to move to Florida with his family, which I already knew very well. I became pregnant that same year. During the entire marriage and relationship, there was always another person involved. I'd known about them and about the child they'd had together prior to the marriage, what I didn't know about was the ongoing relationship they continued to indulge in.

To me, my husband was very handsome. He was strong, smart, and athletic. Prior to our marriage, he had attended Arizona State University and as a result of being one of the top ten in the nation in the 440 hurdles, he had all kinds of sponsors. In addition to all of his other sports accomplishments, he was also headed to the NFL. He had what I now know of as many demons that plagued his life, demons that caused distractions. As a result of those distractions, all of his hopes and dreams went out of the window and after a while he had many regrets, regrets that negatively affected our marriage.

Being indulged by his parents and being indulged as a celebrity college athlete, my husband was accustomed to a certain lifestyle that our marriage did not afford him. The indulgences weren't there, the celebrity adoration wasn't there, and he was struggling to adjust to normal life. That adjustment was the source of many of the issues in our marriage, but I didn't know it then. Hindsight is always 20/20.

After being mistreated, mishandled, and so very hurt and broken by my husband, I took my pregnant self back home to New York where I could have peace of mind and regroup. I had the baby in 1988, and for reasons I don't remember, it wasn't long before my husband arrived in New York as well. I believe my husband loved me, but he really wasn't ready for commitment or marriage. Marriage is not just a boyfriend/girlfriend thing, it's a 'til death do us part deal and he wasn't yet ready or willing to handle that. Because he wasn't ready for that level of commitment, the marriage was tough. I soon realized that he'd come to New York only to break me again and he didn't even know it.

Although my husband left New York, I remained there with my family. I probably didn't see him again until 1995. It was in that year, prior to moving to Georgia, that I filed for divorce and that divorce was finalized. I filed, figuring that since I hadn't seen him in years, I would probably never see him again. However, in 2000, low and behold, we crossed paths and were both very glad to see each other. My gladness was not only for me though, my joy was also because I had a son who needed to see his father.

The happiness that came from seeing one another caused us to spend a lot of time talking on the phone and reconnecting. That reconnecting is what led to us getting back together in 2000. However, from that reuniting in 2000 until 2017 he and I had a very unhealthy relationship. It was all ups and down all of the time. In fact, the only consistent parts of the relationship was that it went up and down and that he cheated. My ex-husband also had anger issues and control issues. If I addressed anything, he would become verbally aggressive, and if he walked out during those discussions, he wouldn't return until days or weeks later. As a result, I learned to stay quiet and to not say anything. I just dealt with the situation the best I could, and for years I allowed myself to be broken by my ex-husband over and over again.

I'm sure that I'm not the only woman that has ever stayed in a bad relationship because I couldn't help who I loved, but the question I should have been asking myself was why? Why did I stay? Well, I stayed because I always had hope. I was sure that after all of that time he would change. He didn't, and eventually I came to realize that the problem in our relationship wasn't really him, because it wasn't him that needed to change, it was me.

Although the relationship was bad, three things developed out of it for me:

1. A prayer life.
2. A love and respect for myself.
3. A true understanding of forgiveness.

Why? Because every time he hurt me, I went to God and grew closer to God.

I cried so much throughout that relationship that God said, "Let me give her a prayer life so that she will learn how to cry out to Me." And I did. I've had a prayer life for many years now and have developed quite a love and relationship with the Father. Through learning to love the Father, I began to love and respect myself. I had to let go and let God. It was not easy, and it did not happen overnight. It was a process, but I made it through!

We all know that with Gods' processes you get broken all over again! And oh, my goodness, I went through it only to get to a place in God where He allowed me to know that I was wonderfully and fearfully made, and that He loved me and had so much more in store for me. God showed me what loved looked like, and not only did He grant me my requests, but He opened doors that I never would have or could have imagined.

My mind began to shift, my thinking shifted, my attitude shifted. Now when there are things that I don't agree with, I voice my thoughts in a tactful manner. God gave me confidence and He is still perfecting that confidence and a boldness in me. I have been praying every morning at 5:30 for years. Through prayer, I've come to understand that there is always purpose behind every trial and affliction we endure. Nothing we go through is for naught. If we never go through anything, how can we help others when they're going through?

Prayer is my mantle, a calling I've been called to do and an anointing that I have been filled with. I've never been loved so much, and this is a love that comes from God. I love and respect myself enough to know what I want in a spouse and what I refuse to tolerate from a spouse. I'm not perfect, so I'm not expecting perfection. However, what I am expecting in a husband is that he first loves God. Then I'm expecting us to have a friendship, to have love, respect, kindness, gentleness, and humility. I'm also expecting him to be a protector and a provider even if I have my own. I do understand that marriage is a partnership and in this partnership I want a husband that will only have eyes for me. I'd like him to be spontaneous, not mean or angry, and to have absolutely no baby mama drama. I want him to have a relationship with God.

When I say I want us to have love, there are four types of love I'm speaking of.

Storge - empathy bond

Phili -friend bond

Eros - romantic love

Agape - unconditional love

A relationship should embrace all four of these types of love, the biggest of which is the unconditional love. God has such unconditional love for His creation that He delivered the children of Israel over and over and over again. Amazing! You can almost feel Gods hurt and disappointments in the Children of Israel as they consistently disobeyed His commandments, as they consistently went against His will. Yes, there were always consequences for their behavior, but God loved them unconditionally and He now loves us unconditionally. We find it hard to continue to forgive over and over, but that's what the Father did and does. No, I'm not God, you're not God.

Sometimes we are not strong enough to love unconditionally, sometimes we intentionally chose not to love unconditionally and that's ok. Everyone's story and journey is not the same.

Forgiveness- psychologists generally define forgiveness as a conscious, deliberate decision to release feelings of resentment or vengeance toward a person or group who has harmed you, regardless of whether they actually deserve your forgiveness or not. The Bible says plenty about forgiveness, "Be kind to one another, tender hearted, forgiving one another, as God in Christ forgave you." Mark 11:25, and "When you stand praying , forgive, if you have anything against anyone, so that your Father which is in heaven may forgive you your trespasses." For the believer, the prayer warrior and intercessor, we must definitely walk in forgiveness.

The word forgiveness can carry a wide range of meaning, especially in the Greek language. It means to remit (a debt), to leave (something or someone) alone, to allow (an action), to leave, to send away, to desert or abandon, and even to divorce. I learned to forgive myself first for allowing those things to happen and for allowing it to go on for so long, and then I forgave him, my ex-husband. It's ironic that as

I forgave, I was no longer hurt by those past experiences. I was no longer angry, no longer asking for revenge, and no longer asking God, "Why me?" Through the true act of forgiveness, I've been healed, delivered, and set free. Hallelujah, what a wonderful feeling! To be at peace with my past is an awesome experience.

How often have we forgiven that family member, that friend girl, that bestie, our children etc., but oftentimes find it difficult to forgive our spouse? Forgiving doesn't mean that you're taking them back or that you're excusing the behavior or the hurt or even that you've forgotten about it. Forgiveness means that you're ok, it means that you've moved beyond the experience. It might have broken you, but it didn't kill you, it only made you better. Forgiveness can lead to feelings of understanding, empathy, and compassion for the one that hurt you. Forgiveness, for me, took me to a place of peace, a kind of peace that helped me to go on with life.

Today, my ex-husband and I are good friends and we talk often. Once forgiveness helped me to heal, I decided that I will never lose my voice again. As a result of having my voice, even now, I'm able to share with him the things that affected me during the marriage and things that have affected me even afterward. We can laugh together, with each other and at each other. We can share our personal sad moments with one another. I've even had to minister to him on many occasions.

This journey has not been easy by far, it was all uphill. There were good times, it wasn't all bad, but when there is a lot of hurt, that hurt can outweigh and overshadow the good. There was purpose in going through what God allowed me to go through within that relationship. I am thankful to have come through it if only to be able to share it with you. The baggage from my previous marriage will not be a part of my next marriage.

I am a wife in waiting and I now know that the best is yet to come!

Praying

Wives

Successfully Married: Ten or Less Years

My Vows

Poetess Kalina Harrison

I vow to let God do His thang and keep my hands out of His plans.
I vow to take myself on a date,
buy myself flowers, give myself a tight hug, ponder
on all of the reasons that I love me, and celebrate
the anniversary of when I became one with God.
The problem is already solved, and I vow to accept
God's Promise for my life.
If it's God's will, then I will be a wife.
Nothing will separate me from the love of Christ
"For He has given me not a Spirit of fear, but of
power and love and self-discipline."
II Timothy 1: 7
I am so glad that when I am faithless
"... He remains faithful; for He cannot deny Himself"
II Timothy 2:13

So, I vow to let go of a limiting mindset and wholly inherit God's Kingdom. There is nothing that God can't do for those who believe in Him.

As I Waited for God's Best

I Delighted Myself in the Lord

Diana L. Morrow

I had been wondering where my Boaz was and why he hadn't shown up yet. I'd had a failed marriage and although I was ready to try again, I had anxiety about it. I often thought that maybe I wasn't good enough, maybe I'd failed as a wife, maybe I was damaged goods, or that I was probably meant to be alone. One day while having a pity party, I had a God encounter. He told me that I needed to first make HIM my husband, and that my Boaz would come in due season. God then led me to a scripture that still ministers to my heart today, "Delight yourself also in the Lord, and He will give you the desires and secret petitions of your heart. Commit your way to the Lord [roll and repose each care of your load on Him]; trust (lean on, rely on, and be confident) also in Him and He will bring it to pass." Ps. 37:4-5. Although I was encouraged, it took me some time to fully understand what "He will give you the desires and secret petitions of your heart" really meant.

In my first marriage, I hadn't included God in my decision-making process and that proved to be a mistake that almost cost me my life since the relationship was a physically and mentally abusive one. God knows what's best for us. If we allow Him, He will place His thoughts in our hearts, and when we become one with Him, His thoughts become our thoughts. When I made God my husband and began to understand all of my insecurities, fears, and doubts, a confident assurance came over me and secured me in the knowledge that God had a great and glorious plan for my life. My Boaz was on his way and I needed to continue preparing myself for my husband.

I Asked God for an Example to Serve

One of the greatest challenges of having a thriving and successful marriage is knowing what that looks like and having an actual live example to guide you. Once I realized this, I asked God to identify a Christian couple that was not just hearers of the word, but doers. And I asked that their doing of the word be reflected in their daily life so that I could see it.

If you grew up in a household with both parents as a demonstration of Christ-like faith, maybe you can skip this step. I, however, grew up in a household with a Christian mother, but not a Christian father. My mother did her best to keep a Christian household, but my father didn't make it easy. He was born-again, but his outward demonstration of how a Christian should behave in general was just not evident.

As a result of growing up in such a household, my first marriage mirrored the marriage of my parents. After my divorce, I knew that I didn't want to get the same result next time around, so I asked God for a Christian example. He knew my heart and He is faithful, therefore He showed me a couple at my church, and I began to watch them like a hawk. I was checking out everything they did. I would see them holding hands while praying, I would see him let her seat down for her at service, I would see them smiling at one another. I was in awe.

They were leaders at our church and always came in super sharp and color coordinated, I loved that about them. One day God told me to go and introduce myself and I froze. Because of my hesitation, I thought that I'd missed my opportunity because for a while I didn't see them anymore. They'd always sat on the second row, the first two seats in the center section. I was devastated, I knew what God had told me to do, yet I'd been disobedient. But thank God for His mercy and His grace, because He presented another opportunity for me to do what He'd asked me to do. Our church began opening up satellite locations all around the country. A friend asked me why I wasn't attending the new satellite that was closer to my home and I told him that I was comfortable attending the main church.

So, let me make this point before continuing, don't be stuck in your way of doing things, be willing to break old habits or you might miss out. Why do I say this? Because a whole year later, I finally decided to check out that satellite church, and guess what?

The couple God had told me to introduce myself to had been made the overseers of that location. I was excited beyond measure!

Long story short, once they saw that I had a heart for prayer, they asked me to lead the Prayer Ministry. We developed a very close relationship, and I became her Armor Bearer. I got exactly what I asked God for, an example I could serve. She taught me what it would take to have a successful marriage. They were both ministers, and when God finally sent my husband, they were the ones that conducted our pre-marital counseling and our ceremony. She is now my most dear friend, today and forever! Thank you Minister's Rosevelt and Princess Lawrence for being the Godly example I needed.

I Almost Settled for Less than God's Best

After my first marriage, before I was really born again, and before God sent my Boaz, I would become anxious, thinking about how things were taking too long. Ten years after my divorce, I had decided that I wanted to be married again and I began dating someone. For several years I thought he was the one, but a dear sister in Christ would always remind me that this relationship wasn't the one that God had for me. However, I would do my best to convince her, and myself, that he was good enough to be my husband. While dating him, I became born-again and told him that the things we used to do, we could do no longer. As I focused even more on the word of God, He would tell me very clearly that this man wasn't the one and that I should shift my thoughts to Him because He was preparing me for my husband. That was how I waited.

I began to declare this prayer over my life daily, *"Thank you, Heavenly Father, that he who finds a wife finds a good thing and obtains favor of the Lord. Thank you for separating, consecrating, and purifying me unto You. Thank You that I deal wisely with all of my affairs. My husband is a man after Your very own heart. He deals wisely with all of his affairs. He is loving, caring, humble, patient, and handsome. He shall find his Queen when he finds me, I will be suitable, adapted, and complementary to him. We shall go about uplifting and building the kingdom of God and living a prosperous life together while dispensing blessings to others. I believe I receive what I have prayed, In Jesus' Name, Amen."*

(Scriptural References: Proverbs 18:22, Habakkuk 2:2, Joshua 1:8 and Genesis 2:18).

That prayer is what kept me steadfast and immovable about the plan and purpose God had for me. He was purging all of the wrong thinking from my past and even though it was for sure a process, the image of His plan for my life was indeed becoming clearer. In fact, it was becoming so clear that in 2001, while waiting on God to send my husband, my spiritual mother, Mother Mitchell, once said to me, "When you meet your husband, you will know him, and you will not date him." I was confused about what she'd said to me, struggling to understand how I could marry someone that I'd never dated. But lo and behold, when God finally did connect me with him, it happened exactly the way she said it would. From her, I learned that even though God wants us to lean on Him and seek Him, He works to keep us from giving up on our journey by connecting us with words of wisdom from our elders to help us along the way. Because of her words, I'm now aware that we should not get weary in well doing. However, if we do, God will send those he speaks through with wisdom that they've learned from Him to keep us moving along our journey.

Being open to the wisdom of the words of elders is actually a blessing from God.

One day while working in the Philippines, a friend from my past replied to a post I'd made on Facebook. We'd been classmates from Pre-K to 8th grade, our parents would carpool us to school until we were old enough to catch the bus. We were so excited to catch each other up on the past thirty years that we were communicating regularly. Turns out we both had been married, both had children, and were both now single. Once, I returned to the States, we continued regular conversation, and right before Valentine's Day, he said the Lord told him I was his wife. By that time, I knew he was my husband, and two months later we were married.

He was God's best for me and I'm so glad that I didn't settle. Six months later, I relocated from Georgia to Spencerport, NY. I'm also glad I was obedient and that through my obedience I put myself in position for the love of my life, my amazing man of God, my rock, and my partner for life, Levern Morrow Jr. to find me!

Write the Vision That God Has given to You

Are you at your wits end, wondering if true love will ever come your way? If so, you should speak him into existence. Everything accomplished in the Kingdom is done by faith. Therefore, put yourself in line to receive your Boaz by faith, through your words, and through obedience to God. Words are the most powerful things in the universe. Everything that exists in the world was created by words. When you understand this principle and you have God in your heart, you will begin to create your husband. Through meditation on God's word, you will become clear on who you really are in Christ, and God will reveal who your husband is. Here is where you have to see him through the lens of God. God said to write the vision and make it plain that they who read it may run with it, Habakkuk 2:2. Trust God with all of your heart! Give him everything, the good, the bad, the ugly. Give Him your shame, your disappointments, your hurts and know that He loves you and has already planned the BEST for you. He already knows everything about you because He created you!

Therefore, as Jeremiah 29:11 states, God knows the thoughts and plans that He has for you, thoughts of good and not evil to bring you to an expected end. Your future is already in God's past! He knows the husband that will find you, so what you must do is come up higher and see as God sees. See your husband through the eyes of God and begin to create him. I've learned that you must have him in the spirit realm before he will show up in the physical.

You might ask how you're going to create him, well, I'd like to show you. I have been passionately facilitating Vision Board Workshops for seventeen years and I have seen many of my dreams come to fruition.

Won't you join me for my next workshop, Praying Wives In Waiting. Once you email Diana@DianaLMorrow.com you will receive details on how to register and what you'll need to prepare.

Until then, might I suggest that you purchase a beautiful heart shaped picture frame, place a picture of yourself and a man of your choosing as a placeholder for your Boaz. Begin to visualize yourself married to him, and pray daily over your lives. You can use the prayer I shared earlier in the chapter, or create one that gets your juices flowing. Share with me your testimonies of what you see changing in your lives. Here's a secret: that's exactly what I did! You'll hear more about that in the workshop.

Remember, God will not withhold any good thing from you, including your husband! Only believe and receive it done by faith, NOW!

My closing prayer for you, beloved daughter, is *Father God, thank You for the promise that You gave to Your daughter that You would give her the desire and secret petition of her heart as she delights herself in You. Thank You, Father that her expectations come from You only. She is complete and established in who she is in You Father, and she shall desire to become one with the man You have prepared for her. She shall fulfill Your divine purpose and plan for their life together as one. She believes and receives that it is so. Be it done unto her according to Your word, In Jesus Name, Amen!*

Hiding in Honesty

Regina McNish

Waking up to the woman I once was, was the hardest thing I could do. While looking at myself in the mirror, I would wonder who I was and what I was supposed to do with myself. I was the little girl that was molested by a family member and a family friend. I was the young teen that did not know her place in life, and that ran with whatever crowd accepted her. I wondered how I was going to hide the young adult inside of me that ran the streets popping pills and smoking marijuana to keep her mind from dealing with her haunting past.

I didn't know how to get rid of the filthy odor of my past even though I so desperately wanted to move on. So, I went to God in prayer for a man to love just me, not the me I had once been, but the me I had become. The saved me. The holier than thou me. The new me. Whatever man God sent into my life could never know the old me. I was going to hide the honesty of the old me inside of the truth that I had become.

Even though I prayed and prayed for God to send me a husband, in my mind I was wondering if I was ready, if I was I capable of loving him the way he needed to be loved. One day, while sitting at home minding my business, I received a phone call about a man who might be interested in meeting me.

"He reminds me of you," she stated.
I agreed to speak with him and advised her to give him my number. I believed I was ready.

Prior to that call, I'd been abstinent for a whole year. I'd stopped doing drugs and had fully committed my life to Christ. Even though I had prayed for a man, I was not actively looking for a man. I was too busy trying to fix me. However, I felt deep in my heart that this upcoming meeting was an act of God. Dismissing the fact that I was still under construction and that I still had some work that needed to be done, I went ahead with talking to him. Months had gone by before we actually began to conversate, and just like a resume, when we finally did talk, I shared all of the wonderful things about me with him. I shared all of the great things about me. I hid all of the honest things about me.

Because we were mostly talking on the phone, of course I couldn't just pour out my dirty laundry over the phone, and when I finally saw him in person, I certainly couldn't share that laundry on our first date. But things moved fast and before I knew it, we had become inseparable! Weekend vibes were everything. I would rush home from work just to get ready for our weekend special. I would clean up real nice and become the woman he was looking for while forgetting the woman that I had been, forgetting the things I had buried inside of me. It wasn't long before I realized that he loved me, and that was all that mattered to me. I was so happy that I would speak life over him and ask God to make him my husband because I had never found a love like that before. I so desperately needed to know that someone could really love me.

Months flew by and it was amazing. My life was filled with public displays of affection, something I never thought I would experience. He was so amazing, he catered to my every need. We quickly moved in together because we knew we were both ready to live our lives together. However, what he didn't know was that from nine to five I would be at work crying, trying so hard to understand and control the hurt and the pain of my past. Then from five until the next day I was the best woman I could be for him.

I would get home, cook dinner, wash clothes, and clean the house. After all of that was done, I would get in bed and make sweet love to him like I had never done before. He wasn't allowed to know my pain, wasn't allowed to see my tears. He couldn't even get a whiff of the stench of my past. Instead of focusing on our intimacy, thoughts of hiding the real me was running through my mind while we made love.

During our relationship, I fell into a major depression and managed to hide even that from him. Life was perfect, at least it looked that way to those on the outside looking in. Family and friends loved our relationship so much that we became "relationship goals". However, we had everyone fooled because he was going through the same issues I was going through!

What I admired about him was that he'd become tired of hiding his past, so he was not afraid to share even though what he had to share was haunting him. I dared not! My resume would remain clean and perfect, I just couldn't risk sharing anything and have him leave me because of what I may have revealed.

However, things don't usually stay hidden for long. Moving forward in our relationship, things began to leak out. We had mutual friends that he used to hang out with and that began to make me mad. I was upset, wondering what would happen if they said something. Every time he would spend any time with them, I would lose my mind wondering what they'd revealed and what he knew about me that I didn't want known. We would argue because I hated the fact that he hung out with them. Suddenly, I became so stressed about being exposed that little things started to bother me. I did not want him to know the old me, the new me was all he needed to know. The new me would be the one he married.

Before we knew it, four years had gone by. In those years we'd struggled a lot. We struggled from losing work, from the repossession of my vehicle.

Then he was injured at work and could not work, so I had to carry the household all by myself. I would cry on the city bus to and from work, asking God if this was what I deserved. I'd stopped making love to him, started denying him of what I introduced him to in the beginning. And with so much hanging over his head, he decided to step out on our relationship. Yes, he cheated on me, but I mean, why not? Why wouldn't he? I wasn't being honest with myself, why would he be honest with me? Nevertheless, I was still devastated. I could not believe he'd done that to me after all I had sacrificed. Needless to say, we split up and I urged him to get out!

"Go, leave me alone," is what I said to him.

After all those years of rejection, I was once again rejected! I believed that if I were the type of woman that would've cursed him out, or the type to go clubbing and ignore my responsibility, he would've appreciated me more. Perhaps if I'd been the woman I used to be, he would've never tried me like that. But I wasn't that woman, and he did try me like that.

It took some time for me to reevaluate my life, but when I did, I came to the conclusion that I could never take the blame for him cheating, but I could take responsibility for my own actions. I went to God once again, just like I'd done the in the beginning. I prayed for weeks, asking Him what I should do. Days and nights all blended into one, they all looked the same to me. Filled with hurt and rejection, I wanted so desperately to run back to the familiar.

A short time later, while in the midst of my prayers, I once again asked God what I should do and how I should move on from there? It was then that I heard a soft voice say, "Love him like I love you."

I knew I loved him, he had already asked for forgiveness, and I had forgiven him before, but I was still undecided. However, when I closed my eyes to picture my future, I only saw him. I understood at that very moment that I was once the young lady that he was currently with. I was once the promiscuous one, going from place to place, and God had loved me unconditionally. In fact, God loved me so much that He'd forgiven me for every single thing I'd done. His grace found a way to clean me up and make me new. Therefore, why should I be afraid of the monsters from my past? God had forgiven me for them. And if God had forgiven me for my monsters, why should I crucify my ex for his own monsters? I couldn't.

As a result of that conversation with God, I spoke with him daily and shared words of affirmation with him. Then I began to do the one thing I had feared the most, I began to share the real me with him. All of me. I opened the door of truth. My truth. Little by little I shared with him, and all of a sudden it was like we had just met. Every time I looked into his eyes, I saw a deeper love for me shining in them. It was completely different from our day one of four years ago.

After months had passed, we decided to start all over. I knew how much people would talk about our decision, but I didn't care. I loved him and I was not ready to let go. This time I was going to get it right. I found a way to open up. When he found out about my molestation, he looked me in my eyes, and as serious as he could be, with everything within him he said, "You never have to worry about that ever happening to you again, or to our children!" Then he hugged me tightly and I melted with tears in his arms. His love had grown deeper! Somehow, the darkest moment of my life was out, and he loved me even more. At that point, I felt deep in my heart that

God had ordained this love and I decided that I would no longer hold myself hostage to my past. From then on, I decided to let it all out.

It was October 2014, a normal date night out on the beach for us. We sat for dinner and were having a great time with one another. I loved that man with every fiber of my being, so much so that every moment seemed to go by in slow motion that night. I didn't want the night to end. After dinner we went for walk on the beach. As we sat watching the beautiful stars and the big bright moon, before I could even absorb the beauty of the night, he got on one knee and asked me to marry him. I knew I would say yes, so I said, "Yes, yes, yes!"

However, I had one request before he slid the ring on my finger. My request was for us to pray. I wanted to invite God into our union simply because I knew it wouldn't work without Him. We prayed, and as we did so, tears rolled down our cheeks. Knowing everything that we had been through, and despite the hurt, the pain, the tears, and the rejection of our past, we were actually willing to move forward together. He chose me and I chose him. Finally, we said our amen and he put the ring on my finger with confidence and pure joy. I could not take my eyes off of my ring. As I stared at the ring, I pictured the old me, the little girl who continuously reminded herself that she was too damaged to love or be loved. But seeing that ring helped me to bury the young lady that forced herself to hate men and to treat them like dirt. After a short while, I smiled. Then I dismissed the thought of the broken woman that had always claimed she would finally get married at fifty because the life she lived was much better than settling down with one guy.

On July 18th, 2015, we said yes. That was the most beautiful day of my life. I was dressed in white, not because I wanted to display purity, but I chose white because in the eyes of God I had been made new. I'd gotten rid of my past by sharing it with the man I loved, the one person that accepted me for me and that I accepted for him. Without any judgment we decided to choose love. Love conquers all, and indeed it helped us to conquer all.

I'm sharing my story because I want to help women free themselves before they decide to open up and be honest, first with themselves and then with others. A lot of what I went through could have been prevented if I had only sat down and faced my demons in the mirror instead of covering them behind the thought of being reborn again in Christ. Yes, the word of the Lord says once you accept Christ as your Lord and savior you are made new, but what if you never really get rid of the old you? You must still look at her in the mirror daily. My husband was told about the old me. He'd never met her and I'm glad he hadn't. As much as I feared him finding out about my past, I am also glad that he knows about the old me because now he knows how to handle the real me.

When you decide to hide in honesty, how will your husband know not to say things that can trigger something that once hurt you? The truth is that he won't know. We all have gone through something, no one has a clean slate. I decided to write my first book, *He Interceded, and* it talks about my life and how God interceded in every situation that was meant to kill me. I know that what I went through prepared me for today. I used to look at my past and it would make me feel unworthy of the love I have today. Now, I see that past as something I had to endure to save someone else's life today.

After my husband read my book for the first time, it hurt him deeply to learn that his wife had gone through so much. However, reading it brought him to a place where he understood my strength even more than he already had. He came to love me even more. My hurt became his hurt, my tears became his tears. And when he made love to me, he was even more passionate. Simply because he understood all of me.

My advice to you is to be honest and to walk in your truth. If he is the one, nothing you did in your past will hinder him from loving and appreciating you in your today. Give yourself time to heal so that when you do meet *the one* you will be ready to be unapologetically you! All of you!

Words of Wisdom
If we claim to have fellowship with Him and yet we walk in the darkness we lie and do not live out the truth. But if we walk in the light, as He is in the light, we have fellowship with one another, and the blood of Jesus, His son purifies us from all sin.
1 John 1:6-7 NIV

This verse exemplifies walking in honesty. It reminds us that if we claim that Jesus is our Lord and Savior, we are in fellowship with Him daily. So, why do we hide our truth? We must walk in our truth because it is who we are. It helps mold us into who we really want to become as wives, as mothers, as a friend. Honesty is not only telling the truth, it's about being real with *YOU*! Its about letting others know who you are and what you want and need to live your authentic life the way God intended it to be. The opposite of honesty is deception, and even though it is not your intention to deceive someone, it is what you are doing. I urge you to walk in your truth. No matter what the outcome is, be your authentic self and let God pull you into the love that He has already set aside just for you.

Regina Mcnish: Married 5 Years

Conflicts that Cause Confusion:

How to Handle the Bad Times of the Vows

Chenique Pinder

As a little girl, I often daydreamed about my wedding day. At that time, marriage from my perspective was a beautifully designed gown that everyone would envy, accented by flawless makeup, and a hairstyle like none other. I envisioned lots of bridesmaids, family, and friends all having a great time, enjoying great food and dancing. The extravagance of the wedding surely made the marriage, or so I thought. And how could it not?

There is a saying, "After the wedding comes the marriage." I have found this to be true. When entering the covenant of marriage, a portion of the wedding vows state "for better or worse". This marital journey has taught me that anyone can endure the good times of the vows, but the bad times of the vows require so much more effort, patience, tolerance, and often selflessness. Remember that the bad times of the vows do not refer to any form of abuse. In this chapter, I will discuss a few challenges that I had to face and overcome as a married woman.

Financial Challenges

Financial challenges in a marriage can create difficulties. This challenge can either stem from poor choices, or from circumstances that are beyond your control. In my personal situation, the greater reason for our financial issues was due to circumstances beyond our control. However, there were also some poor decisions made.

When my husband and I married, we never imagined that a circumstance would arise where only one of us would be able to work. When that situation hit, however, it felt as though we went from a two-income home to a one income home overnight. This was extremely difficult and required us to be disciplined. Being disciplined for me was a challenge because I was used to getting my hair and nails done every two weeks. I was used to shopping and purchasing things that I honestly did not need but wanted. To make matters worse, I had just given birth to our third child, and first daughter. This was simply not a good time for us to lose any resources.

I wondered how it would be possible to care for three children in addition to ourselves with only one income. At first, I was resistant to our new normal and was not willing to sacrifice the things I had grown accustomed to prior to and during our marriage. My husband managed money best and was always looking for the best deals and the best possible ways for us to save. I, on the other hand, was accustomed to spending as soon as we got it, and this caused tension in our marriage because we were no longer in a position where I could splurge or spend unnecessarily. We would have major arguments because I associated the strictness that my husband had with money to him treating me as if I were a child. During many heated arguments I would yell, "I am not a child, I am a grown woman!" The fact was that I *was* a grown woman, but I was not making responsible financial decisions.

We had to endure the season of one consistent income for many years before I finally came to the realization that my poor spending habits had to be controlled. We had to create a budget and cut unnecessary expenses to ensure we were able to provide for our family. My husband also had to make sacrifices. He loved buying nice clothes, but because he entered a different season, he had to learn to be even more content with what he had.

Financial challenges can make or break a marriage. I am happy to say that those challenges have made our marriage. It allowed us to put things into perspective. Through this, we realized that the things we thought we needed when money was in the bank were not really needs but wants. We had to learn to compromise and to make decisions that were in the best interest of the entire family and not just one person. Those sacrifices were for the greater good.

In seasons of financial hardship, God was teaching us a lesson and that lesson was how to be a good steward over money. Those were principles we were not taught as children, so we had to take that journey of learning together for the greater good of our marriage and our family, and so that we could secure our future. Those seasons of financial hardships taught us lessons that we would never forget.

Being A Married Friend

The transition from being a single friend to a married friend was particularly challenging for me as a wife. Prior to marriage, I was accustomed to talking on the phone with my friends whenever I wanted and with no time constraints. I went places with friends as frequently as I wanted without having to share the details with anyone outside of that circle.

I recall one of our very first marital arguments, I had just gotten home from a long workday. When I arrived home, I was on the phone with a friend engaging in a conversation that had started from the moment I left the office. At that point, we were about thirty minutes into our conversation and that conversation lasted for another two hours. After hanging up, I noticed my husband seemed upset, so I asked him what the problem was. He began to share how he felt it was unfair that I'd spent two hours on the phone after walking in the house and that I had been so engulfed in the conversation that I'd barely acknowledged him.

By the time he finished spewing his dislike of what occurred, I was fuming. So, when it was my time to speak, I completely lost it. I recall telling him how the individual was my friend and that I would talk to her anytime I chose to and for as long as I wanted to. Those words made matters worse. In that moment, I did not see anything wrong with what I had done or said. In all honesty, I did not see or understand what the issue was.

Those behaviors continued for some time because I simply could not understand the problem. This began to cause friction and distance in our relationship. It was only then that I realized I had to reevaluate the situation, I did not want to lose my marriage because of that. I had to seek the Holy Spirit for wisdom and insight into my behavior.

The problem was that I was married but still behaving like I was single. I had to realize that my role had changed from a single friend to a married friend and there were changes that came with that. It was not that my husband wanted to control me, he only wanted to spend time with me, but my time had been occupied by my friends. The trouble was also not in talking to my friends, it was how that talking was being done. When I walked into our home, which was our sanctuary, my husband should've had my undivided attention. Those were intimate moments where we talked about our day and where we released any frustrations from that day. It was moments where we both encouraged and prayed for each other. It was ok to speak with my friends, marriage did not have to change that, but I had to prioritize.

As a result, I adjusted and decided to catch up with my friends on the way to work, on the weekends, or at other times that were convenient. Spending time with my spouse and children had to be a priority, and I committed myself to not placing them second to anyone or anything. This took time and work, but today I can honestly say that I have found that balance between being a wife, being a mother, and being a married friend. My friends, whether married or single, understand that God is first, and then my family is my priority. Their friendship is a priority as well, but not above my family. Real friends will understand that and respect the changes that occur with that. Any friend that does not understand that is not a friend to have.

You should never be placed in a position where you must choose between a friend and your marriage. If by any chance you do find yourself in such a position, my advice to you is to choose wisely.

Respect and boundaries are critical to the success of a marriage. You set the precedence and what you do others will follow. You must demand respect for your spouse and your marriage, and this must be made clear from the inception. In many instances, family and friends mean us well, but there are times where one or the other may get out of character and become disrespectful to your spouse. When this happens, deal with it immediately.

Early on in our marriage, I had a friend who got into an argument with my husband. The argument got out of hand and she became very disrespectful. That was where I, as his wife, had to step in. I let her know that I would not sit and allow her to disrespect my husband. That was not received well by her. She placed a wedge in our relationship, and it became strenuous. Her belief was that I had allowed my husband to come in and destroy our friendship. Even after talking the situation through with her, after some time expired, it was obvious that she could not get over what happened. Sadly, I had to make the decision to end the friendship. This was a very difficult decision because she walked beside me through some very difficult life situations, but I knew that based on her stance, the friendship could no longer flourish.

It was not that I didn't love my friend, it was the fact that I realized I would always be placed in a position of choosing, and that would open the door to a reoccurrence of the disrespect. Respect and boundaries go hand in hand, and you must set boundaries for your marriage. You tell people what they can or cannot do and what you will or will not accept. If there are no boundaries, people will do as they please. Crossed boundaries is also a breeding ground for disrespect.

Remember, you did not marry you or your spouse's family and friends, you married your spouse. Make it crystal clear what your expectations are and the consequences for doing the opposite of your expectations. Set healthy boundaries, do not allow your friends and family to have a say in your marriage. Do not allow them to control your marriage or be manipulative in your marriage. My family and friends know that disrespect and crossed boundaries are immediately addressed. You cannot hold others to expectations that have not been communicated. Be intentional about setting healthy boundaries.

My greatest advice to you is to always remember why you fell in love with your spouse. Allow that love to be fortified in the difficult seasons of your marriage "Love covers a multitude of sin." 1 Peter 4:8. Be open to make adjustments that will prove vital to the success of your marriage. Remember to always keep God at the center of your marriage. Invite the Holy Spirit into your marriage and allow Him to be the driving force behind every decision and action. I cannot say that it will be easy, but the journey will be worth it. A cord of three strands, God, you, and your spouse, is not easily broken.

Allow Him to Be the Head

T. Lewis-English

But I want you to understand that the head of every Man is Christ, The head of a wife is her husband and the head of Christ...
1 Corinthians 11:13

Before marriage, I'd been taught to be a strong minded, independent woman. I was used to providing for myself and used to managing my finances all on my own. I'd fought hard to get through nursing school and even though I wasn't the best at saving money, I'd made money and I spent it how I wanted.

After I got married, I struggled with allowing my husband, Eddie, also known as Flipp, to lead us. I was a firm believer that my husband should submit to God in order for me to submit to him. I was of the mindset that if he wasn't hearing from God for the next step in our lives, how could I possibly follow him? And when it came to finances, I believed that my money was my money and his money was his money.

Now, don't get me wrong, I knew what Flipp's finances, his past, and his walk with Jesus was before we got married and they didn't quite line up the way they should have. However, even with me knowing things with Flipp weren't in line with God, I still knew without a shadow of doubt that God had told me that he was my husband. I also knew, as well as he did, that there was a greater calling on my husband's life. He was called to preach Gods word and because I knew that, I was able to prepare myself for the fight. Yet, I was still confident that God had told me he was my husband.

I had always been the bread winner and always worked massive hours because that's what I was used to doing. Because I was accustomed to doing those things for myself, I was of the impression that

I was the head of me. Here's where the problem came in; I was out of order. I wasn't doing my wifely duties of allowing my husband to be the head of our family and of our lives.

We'd hit a really rough patch and it looked like we just weren't going to make it. We started going to marital counseling with the Bishop and he, the Bishop, said so many things in those counseling sessions that checked me. Bishop said, "When you get married it's no longer I, it's we, us, and ours." Instantly, my eyes opened. No matter how much money either of us made, we were one. I had to adjust my mindset to understand that if one had, we both had. I needed to learn how to play my position.

I stated before that I'd known what Flipp's walk with Jesus was, but I really didn't. In my mind, because he wasn't praying out loud and in front of me, he wasn't praying at all. And because he didn't talk about God, I felt that he didn't really know Him like he said he did. Oh, was I wrong! At some of the lowest times in my life, it was his prayers and his faith that carried us through. I had to learn to stop putting him down even though I wasn't doing it intentionally. We, as women, can destroy a man and his manhood by the things we say to them or by our actions toward them. Instead of putting him down, had to learn to stroke his ego. There were things that he was very good at and I needed to make sure he knew how much I appreciated him and all that he did to lead our family closer to Christ.

Once I learned that my husband was the head and I began to pray about the things I didn't agree with while allowing God to fix them, submitting to my husband became a little easier for me. Like I said, we had more rough patches than I feel was fair in that short three year period. Some of those situations I felt were unfair to me and I had no intention of moving forward, but I soon learned that words do hurt and that men have feelings as well.

Throughout my journey, I have found that if I trust God and allow Him to work on Flipp, then he would be the husband I needed him to be and in turn God would work on me so that I could be the wife Flipp needed me to be.

Christ used marriage as a symbol of how He loved the church. In order for a marriage to work, God has to be the center of our lives. If I could leave one thing with you, it would be that if you are confident that this is who God has ordained as your life mate, as your husband, be confident enough to follow his lead.

Prayer:

Father, in the mighty name of Jesus, I come to You thanking You for the trials and the tribulations that allowed me to get to where I am today. I ask that you grant these precious wives in waiting the mindset to allow their future husbands to be the head of their families. God, give them husbands who have already committed and submitted themselves to you so that submitting to their own husbands may come easy. We thank You for these wives and their husbands. I pray successful, healthy marriages over them as well as longevity and prosperity. Shape them and mold them individually and then as one. We thank You and we praise You in advance for the connection between husband and wife.

In Jesus name we pray, amen.

Praying

Wives

Successfully Married:
Eleven + Years

Never Enough

Poetess August Love

If I never told you I'm telling you now.
Your love was never enough.

I always yearned for more. Like a half empty
stomach in front of an empty plate.

What you had was never enough.

I suffered in silence like a victim without speech.
You deprived me, a plane with no fuel. You
abandoned me like a childless parent.

I knew from the beginning I would be unsatisfied,
that you could never fill my cup. That you would
never be enough.

I knew I would love you and suffer all the while.

Your effort trumped my unfulfilled soul. I latched on to you as you depleted my being.

I feared without me you would not prevail.

I stroked your ego and blessed all of your dreams.

I dimmed my own light so your light could beam.

In retrospect I now know that I was so wrong to make myself weak so you could be strong.

I poured into you as you drained from me.

I wish I knew then what I know now. I swam in you and now I have drowned.

Worthy of the Wait & Knowing That You Are

Veigh Floyd

More that twenty-one years ago, I was a praying wife in waiting. Waiting on God to bless me with the husband that I'd prayed about and the one He wanted for me. Waiting on my intended to prepare himself to be the husband that I needed, and that God designed to fit me perfectly. Having no idea who this man was, I was willing to wait on him. God had already told me that he was preparing him, and I knew that he would be worth the wait. When God does a thing; He does it well! Knowing this, patience was my portion while God did His work. Of course there was pressure to be married by a certain age, or the fact that everyone around me was married or getting married, the inevitable "when are you getting married?" question haunted me on every occasion; or just by the plain nagging of my grandmother! I watched others as they approached the alter to exclaim "I Do", only to divorce a few short years later; or be forced to live in a situation with a man which she sincerely regretted. She would try for years to work through issues because she wanted to the relationship to work, but to no avail. Others would hang on to the marriage because of the fear of failure and having to admit that she should have waited.

These types of scenarios played over and over again in the headlines, on the movie screen, and in real life situations, and I wanted no part of it. I was therefore content to get it right the first time. If it took a little longer- fine; my desire to not repeat the process was greater than my desire to beat the wedding clock. As wives in waiting, our priority is to be in prayer that your future husband is seeking Christ and making Him first in his life.

But seek first his kingdom and his righteousness,
and all these things will be given to you as well
Matthew 6:33

You are His Favor

Whether you are a wife or a wife in waiting, it is important that you first understand that a wife is her husband's favor. We as women must remember that what we bring to the table in a marriage is equally as important and sometimes more important than what our husband may bring because we are "bearers". We carry, uphold, and bring things forth. We carry and bear children. Some women are even the backbone for their husbands who lean on them heavily for support in jobs and in ministry.

In some relationships, women set the tone. We establish the setting emotionally, atmospherically, and even economically for the home and for the family. Good women set the atmosphere for the home, and the rest of the family. She gives her husband a place to lay his head. Even if a woman is a leader in her own right, she can simultaneously be a help meet for her husband. Women who are focused and intentional can bring out the best in a man. Even with a man that is unsure of his own destiny, if he builds a relationship with the right woman, she will usually encourage him to align his goals and reach for his greatest potential. She will assist and encourage him, and then cheer him on, as he accomplishes his goals for success.

She is his favor and makes his life more favorable. She will pray for him and go to God on his behalf. A good wife will respect him and ensure that he is well represented and presented in a favorable light. She will challenge him and offer proper perspective. She will transform the house that he provides into a home. The bible talks about this woman in Proverbs 31. She is often referred to as the "*Woman with Notable Character*" Proverbs 31:10-31.

He that finds a wife finds a good thing and obtains favor of the Lord.

Proverbs 18:22

It is not good that the man should be alone; I will make him an help meet for him.

Genesis 2:18

You Are Fearfully and Wonderfully Made

There are so many details in the book of Psalms that let us know how much the Lord loves us, and the particularly close attention He pays to every one of us. He has searched us all and He knows everything about us. He knows when we rise and when we lie down. He knows our thoughts and our very words before we even speak them. His knowledge of us far exceeds what we can even comprehend. We cannot hide from Him no matter where we go, He is everywhere. He can even see through darkness because He is light, no darkness can dwell where He is. He knew us before we were born and knit us together in our mother's womb. That is a true testament to the attention He pays to us, and how much He wants to know us. Not only that, but it also lets us know how much He wants us to succeed.

Now, if God takes the time to know you so personally and intricately, how much more important is it for you to know yourself? The bible says that "You are fearfully and wonderfully made." He searches you out and knows your path. What an extreme compliment to know that your Heavenly father cares enough about you to search you out!

Embrace the fact that the Lord thinks you are so special that He takes His time to look for you and to know all about you.

Before you can attach yourself to someone else in Holy matrimony, you must first know who you are. You must know how you excel and what your limitations are. You must know how effectively you communicate, and you must know what your triggers are. Do you clam up during a disagreement, or do you express you concerns clearly? Do you share freely or are you selfish? Are you domestic or could you use some training in that area? Are you fiercely independent or indecisive? Are you willing to compromise or are you a controlling?

How well do you know yourself? Are you willing to be honest even if you find areas that you can work on? If you find yourself in any of the descriptions above, the first thing you should know is that you are still awesome! However, everyone can improve in one area or another. No one is perfect. Don't be alarmed or ashamed to find that you too can benefit from growth of some kind. It is really good to know who and how you are so that your intended (husband) can know you as well and so that you two can decide together whether or not you are a good match. It is only fair to give him the same option to choose that you want him to give you. If we took the same care and interest in knowing ourselves the way that God does, we could do exponential exploits for the kingdom, for our families, and for ourselves.

I will praise thee; for I am fearfully and wonderfully made; marvelous are thy works; and that my soul knows right well.

Psalm 139:14

Your Father Calls You Worthy

Women, The Creator of the universe has masterfully handcrafted your frame and being and when He was finished, He declared that it was good! When God places a description on you, it is what He says it is! Whatever He declares you are is what you are and no one can change that. You are a treasure in an earthen vessel. You are a priceless gift and there is limitless value placed upon you. There is no one else alive who is like you. No one else has your

DNA or your fingerprint. Those things are uniquely yours and neither they nor you can be duplicated.

According to research, not even identical twins are one hundred percent alike. They do not have the same fingerprints. You are wo-man, a man with a womb. Through your body passes human life into existence on earth, and that gift alone makes you super- human and fascinating all together! You are one of God's greatest creations.

With that said, it has therefore been established how wonderful and unique you are. You must declare your own value and not let anything, or anyone devalue you. The value of an item is usually determined by what the purchaser is willing to pay for it. God determined that His only begotten Son was a fair price. In this instance, I want you to think of yourself as a one of a kind, extremely rare jewel that will never be mined by others or found on earth anywhere at any time. You get to determine your worth. As much as I feel that everyone should esteem themselves very highly without conceit or haughtiness, not everyone feels that they are valuable. God could have scrapped us and started over, but He found us valuable enough to redeem us. The Lord thought enough of you to come and get you, and to save you from the snare of the enemy. Now, that is priceless!

Before I formed thee in the womb, I knew you; and before you were born I set you apart, and I ordained thee a prophet unto the nations

Jeremiah 1:5

A Worthy Man Protects Your Worth

Some single women feel that they must go to major extremes when dating men. A popular thought process is that a woman must give everything she has and everything she is to prove to a man that she is serious about the relationship.

Now, listen closely women, most men *do not* confuse physical intimacy and love. To most men, these are two totally unrelated issues. Most men do not tie the two together, that is not how they reason or think. Some men can be intimate with women and not be remotely interested in love. A lot of women, on the other hand, associate the two closely together. The reason that most women are physically intimate with a man is because she loves him. The two are inter-related, and indistinguishable. That is a major reason why women should not begin a relationship with intimacy. It is too personal, too deep, and too emotional to engage in too soon. You are giving away the greatest gift that you have. A man should earn the privilege to be in your presence and have your attention. You are precious jewels, pearls, and much too valuable to be trampled upon.

I'm sharing this perspective with you because I want you to understand that learning about a person is important and takes time. It takes time to discover whether or not you really share the same morals and values. Saying that you do and actually sharing the same values are two different things. I want to share with you that good men have standards as well and that you should be able to witness and detect these values and standards; so should every good woman who is interested in pursuing a committed relationship.

There should be standards, non-negotiables, and deal-breakers. Good men understand and respect a woman who has standards from which she will not deviate. He will wait for you, be patient with you, and resist the urge to tempt you to go against the standards you have set. If on the other hand he feels you are his intended (wife) and he has waited long enough, he will ask for your hand in marriage. This is not always the way or sequence in which many relationships go, but so that you understand what a good man looks like, I give this example of the path of a man who is worthy of your time, attention, and hand in marriage. A man who is the opposite, who is pushy, aggressive, and dismissive of your feelings or standards, and who uses this type of behavior to issue you an ultimatum is a man that should be given the curb-side service. In other words, kick him to the curb, speed off, and do not look back! If you remain with him, his actions and the consequences thereof will eventually bleed into other areas of your life together.

Love is patient, love is kind, it does not envy, it does not boast, it is not proud. It does not dishonor others, it is not self-seeking, it is not easily angered, it keeps no record of wrongs. Love does not delight in evil but rejoices with the truth. It always protects, always trusts, always hopes, always perseveres. Love never fails.

1 Corinthians 13: 4-8

You are Worth the Wait; Work While You Wait

Time waits for no one, it is fleeting at best. It seems to slow down when you are suffering, and it seems to speed up when you are enjoying it the most. Where does it go? How do we lose track of it so easily? Why can't we get it back or make it up along the way? I pose these questions because jumping ahead of God and letting your biological clock direct your reasoning, or letting your own understanding of timing guide you, may cause you to set yourself up for a disaster that will take longer than you can fathom to recover from. Don't ever let age or a ticking time clock fool you into making a life choice that you will regret.

I urge you not to decide to have a relationship with, or to marry someone because people are pressuring you or causing you to feel inadequate about yourself. This is *your* life and *you* will have to deal with the consequences of choosing the wrong mate or situation to be in. Take your time, be selective, and seek God alone to make these types of decisions. People will pressure you, but will be nowhere around when you need a means of escape. And when you do reach out for help, the best they can do after they've pressured you into a bad situation is "pray for you".

You are worth the wait and must oversee your own destiny. You must realize that you alone have to live with the choices you make. It doesn't matter what others call you, whether it be single, or alone, don't worry yourself with what everyone else is doing, or how many times you are a bridesmaid. Ask God for wisdom, look for certain characteristics, and do not deviate from any of your pre-set non-negotiables. Know exactly what it is you want in the man you will live with for the rest of your life. Let no one choose that for you but God.

Women, loneliness is the absence of people, but I have discovered that you can be in a room full of people and still be lonely, especially when you don't relate to the people in the room. Aloneness or feeling that you are alone is the absence of purpose. We as women should strive to find our purpose while we are still single. Although this is not the case for everyone, this is what I'd like to emphasize from what I've learned. In a man's quest to find his intended (wife), let him find you doing something. Purpose keeps you busy until he shows up, it also alerts him that there is more to you than meets the eye. And most importantly, it shows him that you are not just twiddling your thumbs while waiting around to be found.

Trust in the Lord with all your heart and lean not to your own understanding; in all your ways acknowledge God and He will direct your path.

Proverbs 3:5-6

God Loves Us......

God loves us so much that He gives us the freedom to choose. He would much rather that we seek Him especially as it pertains to important decisions such as choosing a mate. Remember that God's perfect timing is best. Do not let the opinions of others, your body clock, or some magazine article entice you to move ahead of the timing of God. In your waiting get to know God, seek Him, strengthen your relationship with Him so that you may know His perfect will for your life.

For I know the plans I have for you, declares the Lord, 'plans to prosper you and not harm you, plans to give you hope and a future.

Jeremiah 29:11

Veigh Floyd: Married 21 year

Benefits of Keeping Marriage First

Wynsome S. McLean

The request of the toll attendant jolted me back into reality. "That will be $1.60."

I frantically rummaged through my purse to find some quarters. It was 9:20 on Monday evening and I was just exiting the turnpike for my last ten minutes in the car before I arrived home. I'd left home at 8:30 Monday morning, worked eight hours in Riviera Beach at my nine to five office, then headed straight to Plantation Florida, about one hour away, to see four clients back to back.

Exhausted does not begin to describe how I felt. Being physically and emotionally drained had become a part of my manic Monday experience. As a result, I just wanted to go home, take a shower, and go to sleep. I really didn't want to talk to another breathing soul until 7:30 Tuesday morning. There was only one problem, and it was a big problem. I have a whole husband at home, a living breathing husband, who requires my time and attention. He too had had a long day and I was sure that the caress of his wife would have been well appreciated. A, "How was your day?" with the intention of listening and engaging would have been nice. However, he had gotten used to me walking into the house, mumbling a hello with an occasional lackluster and impassionate grandma kiss before heading to my room.

Proverbs 31:10-12 Amplified Bible (AMP) states:

An excellent woman [one who is spiritual, capable, intelligent, and virtuous], who is he who can find her? Her value is more precious than jewels and her worth is far above rubies or pearls. The heart of her husband trusts in her [with secure confidence]. And he will have no lack of gain. She comforts, encourages, and does him only good and not evil. All the days of her life.

In my pursuit to build a business, to have an engaging ministry, and to be a support for others, the heart of my husband was struggling to trust in me because he really couldn't find my heart. I was so busy connecting to corporations, businesses, clients, saints, etc., that I had violated the first law of marriage. The law of priority. My pursuit of growing businesses became my side dude and I was guilty of misplaced priority. Talk about the need to repent and turn.

Keeping marriage first is God's design.

According to Genesis 2:24, *That is why a man leaves his father and mother and is united to his wife, and they become one flesh.*

When God designed the marriage covenant, He did so with the intent that this special commitment between a man and a woman would be more important than any other human relationship. That is the reason God commanded a man to leave his father and mother for the cause of marriage.

It can then be concluded that leaving father and mother for the sake of marriage wasn't just for Adam and Eve, because they didn't have mothers or fathers. They were created directly by God Himself. Those words were spoken to establish a universal, permanent law of marriage for all people and all times.

Some will say that we become one flesh once we say, "I Do." However, I will submit to you that becoming one flesh is an ongoing, continuous process that matures as we continue to ensure that no other relationship, second to our relationship with Christ, takes priority. We must be one flesh when the babies begin to arrive, when we have a miscarriage, when there is an unfavorable diagnosis, when we get promoted on our job. No other relationship should come before our marriage. Yes, even your children should not come before marriage. Please note that children are your temporary assignment. Once they leave for college or walk down the aisle, they do not want you to go with them. After they've left home, you will be left with the person you neglected for years and years, ready to divorce because the years of misplaced priority has taken its toll on the relationship.

So how do I prioritize my marriage? How do I continue to keep first things first?

The first thing that I had to do was consider what my priorities were, and in what order they fell. I had to reprioritize my entire life to ensure that there was no confusion as to where my priorities lay. Personally, if I had not reconciled the "why" behind the behaviors that I engaged in, those behavioral patterns would be short-lived and not a consistent priority. My "why" for changing my behavior, was to minimize neglect, the neglect of my husband. The further I moved away from my husband, the more likely it became for me to dismiss his needs and overlook the changes that he was experiencing.

Neglect is defined as failing to care for properly, or the state or fact of being uncared for.

A consistent comment that I would get from my clients was their appreciation of how I was able to create space for them to express themselves without judgment. What an indictment towards me for not creating the same space for my number one priority, the ministry I had been given authority to govern. My Marriage.

My husbands' love languages are physical touch, quality time, and words of affirmation. Consequently, I had to learn my husband's personal preferences of expressing love. His expression of quality time usually included a good movie, shoot um up bang bang is his preference. So, whenever I hear "What are we watching?" that is code to take a nap, to take a bath, and to get myself ready for the movie because there is a need for quality time.

I have learned that competition interferes with intimacy. If your partner feels ignored throughout the course of the day, if they feel that they are competing with children, business, ministry, and then when the sun goes down you want to rub upon them, you may be faced with resistance. Making love is an all-day activity that requires intentionality.

I employ emotional intelligence in order to place boundaries around the priority that I give to my marriage. Emotional intelligence is the capacity to be aware of, to control, to express one's emotions, and to handle interpersonal relationships judiciously and empathetically. Emotional intelligence is not *only* needed for me to be able to empathetically connect with my husband. More importantly, it is needed to help me keep a pulse on my feelings of being overwhelmed so that I can be present and available to connect intimately, experientially, emotionally, intellectually, and sexually.

To summarize, a simple formula to follow in order to prioritize your marriage is to assess your priority of marriage in light of God's word. Once you have given your marriage the place that it deserves, create a plan on how you will practically act on this priority. Check-in with your partner, it's okay to ask how you are doing. And remember, it is important to check in often as love languages change or modify over time. Therefore, what you did yesterday may not always work for today.

My G.A.P.

Mia Roan

The G.A.P. years, the Growing, Adjusting, and Progressing years, are seasonal, and ever changing.

I believe the time of my G.A.P. years were designed for me to spend with my Creator, getting to know the wonderful creation predestined as me. This time should have been set aside and set apart for uncovering, through revelation, the masterpiece named Mia.

When it comes to time, I now know that back then I didn't spend the time God had given me correctly. However, in my current season of life, I realize that no matter how you spend time, it will get spent, and there is no refund if you mishandled or wasted it. A refund gives you back only what you paid. For example, $9.99 only returns to you $9.99. In this world, if you don't invest your time wisely, you get no return on that investment at all. Therefore, I thank God for the promise of redemption even with time.

It was in the '80's that I'd planned to join the Air Force Reserve and contemplated studying corporate law because I desired to lead hostile takeovers of well established companies. I'd planned to be self-sufficient, that was my goal. I wanted to spend my time and my money my way, I did not want to share. Not that there were many married couples in my circle at the age of thirteen, but I recognized very early on that you had to share everything with children and with men, and this sharing included your time, you talent, your space, and the list goes on and on.

I did not know at age fourteen that the power of life and death resided in my tongue. I can recall saying to the Lord, "If you are going to bless me with children, it needs to occur before age twenty." Looking back, I now realize that it sounded like I was saying, "God, I dare you."

However, the enemy was listening as well, and he said, "I'll help you." I'd made that statement while not understanding the power of my tongue and its prophecy into my life. I did not *really* plan to have children. Therefore, I thought I was only being funny because I had already planned my time, but choices and consequences have a way of creeping in.

Yes, I chose to have sex as a teen and to get married. However, my only consideration of the consequences of those actions was me wondering, "How hard can it be?" I was encouraged by others, especially the church folk, that marriage was the right thing to do. "Mia, you are so mature for your age," they said. Yes, I was mature, yet, I was not grown up. I had not had enough adult experiences in my life to make truly informed adult decisions. So, I used the knowledge I had back then to make my choice, then I quickly realized that Mrs. Carol Brady had Alice the maid, the Jefferson's had Florence, and all I had were two hands, two feet, and the awakening that I did not marry George Jefferson or Mike Brady. I married a smart, young, black man from a small town in Alabama. He had been raised by a single mother and he fully lacked positive male role models in his life.

Married, I was, not knowing that I was actually supposed to be in my season of singleness, the season of realizing the gem God created me to be. The Encarta dictionary describes a gem as somebody or something considered to be valuable, useful, or beautiful. My season of singleness was designed to teach me my value, my beauty, my purpose, and to teach me about developing a relationship with God. It was designed for me to learn about becoming the bride of Christ all before I became a wife or a mother. My choices, however, took me on a different path.

My path became one that was necessary for life, but it distracted me from my purpose. Well, you only know what you know and sometimes you don't even apply that. I didn't imagine how hard it would be to cook dinner, go to school, do homework, change diapers, go to work, pay bills, etc. Why? Because my imagination had a maid, but my reality had my two hands, my two feet, and my stank attitude. Life was not a thirty-minute sitcom. My reality had to issue constant reminders for me to take out the trash, to be mindful of balancing the checking account, to me remind me of my responsibilities as a car owner, to take care of car repairs, to never leave the gas tank on empty, blah, blah, blah. The list went on and on and thus my stank attitude.

By the age of forty, I looked good on the outside, but I did not feel good on the inside. I was shocked and confused as to how I had lost the focus I'd had in the beginning. I realized that I'd been married more than half of my life. I was born a daughter, yet I had been awarded many titles, sister, student, friend, rebellious, mean, saved by grace, pregnant by sixteen, which afforded me the gracious title of mother. I'd gotten married at **eighteen** and got the title and responsibilities of a wife, add to that stepmom, daughter-in-law, sister-in-law, mother of a child with challenges (multiply handicapped was the 1980's label provided), and list grew.

The years continued to pass and the labels of me kept changing and growing, including but not limited to full-time employee, homework assistant, college student, car owner, bill payer, homeowner, supervisor, carpool driver, grandmother, and even enemy. Knowing that I had been someone's enemy had me facing the reality of me. Well, even though I believe that at some point everyone has been the face of the enemy to someone else, be it through words, actions, deeds, thought, by choice, or by default, I just never thought I would be considered someone's enemy. However, I was.

The realization that half of my life had been spent as married woman and a mom wasn't the most uncomfortable thought, but if I had one redo it, I would allow myself time to live with just me. I would give myself time to get in touch with me without responsibility for others. I went from living with my mother, my sisters, and my children, to residing with my husband and our children. Of course, I continued to develop in the G.A.P. seasons and growth did occur. Yet, when pouring from a half full cup, the obligation to nurture my husband and children left little energy for self. I needed time to dwell, a season of allowing my own cup to be filled and refilled, and to have the ability to pour into the lives of others without such energy robbing adult responsibilities.

But God, in His faithfulness, never gave up on me, and true growth and maturity began to settle in my cup. My cup is now filling and refilling with the Word, attitude, and Spirit of the Lord. I am now able to pour out in a way that previously came in short spurts. I now understand that the labels of me are gems and jewels added to the "crown of me", and I am continually discarding imitation stones for they never quite fit as their source was from the deceiver. Genuine additions to my crown should and do come from surrender to Christ, from Christ's guidance, and from the fruit of the Spirit that allows me to display the godly woman, the kingdom child that is ready to walk in her predestined purpose. By God's Grace I am She and She is Me.

Wives, I pray the soil of your souls will be enriched with the Word of God and your inner beauty will overflow with faith.

Heavenly Father,
You are almighty and powerful; the heavens
declare your glory.
(Psalm 19:1)
Father, may your power rest rule and abide in each praying wife. May she glean from you and continually pour into herself and her husband. May they each check their pride and independence at your throne of grace and begin depending on you as source and savior. May their souls align with your Holy Spirit and the two become one.

In Jesus Name
Amen.
(1 Peter 3:1-5 [NLT], 1 Peter 3:1-5 [TPT])

God's Vision Prevails

Poetess Kalina Harrison

God told me to write the Vision and make it plain,
But Life's expectations clouded my dreams. I know
that God's Word will never come back void,
But what do I do when the things I see overshadow
His voice?

Does Ephesians 3:20 really apply to me?

I know better than to question God's Word, so I
read, "Now to Him who is able to do immeasurably
more than all we ask or imagine according to the
power that worketh in us..."

Sometimes all I can fathom is a life of lonely nights,

Then I ask God the fate of my future; God, is it bright? He affirms,

"For I know the plans I have for you," declares the Lord, "plans to prosper you and not harm you, plans to give you hope and a future."
Jeremiah 29:11

At that moment, the anticipation of lonely nights was replaced with everlasting faith,
For, if God remembered to give the sun to the moon
I am sure He has a divine love awaiting me soon.

Poetess Kalina Harrison

Releasing the Trauma of Yester-Year

Audrey Brooks

What is wrong with me? Will I ever find love? Why did God allow this to happen to me? Where did I go wrong? These are some of the questions many women ask themselves when struggling to release the trauma of yesteryear. For the purpose of this chapter, I need you as the reader to imagine struggling for thirty years with pain from the past, spending day after day praying and hoping the pain subsides. But it does not, at least not for a very long time.

Hello, I am Audrey Brooks, and I am a survivor of yesteryear trauma. I have struggled for thirty years to let go of the experience that held me hostage both mentally and spiritually. My heart and mind could not let go of that trauma and I often wondered if the pain would forever be connected to me. As a result of those questions and of the pain I was suffering, I recognized that I needed counseling and I sought it. Finally, after going to the counseling and coming to terms with some things, I accepted the need for help and took the steps required to release the hurt. No longer did I want to inflict my pain on my family, I wanted to heal, and I wanted to do so not only for myself but for my family as well. I realized that I had a choice to either continue living in the old or to embrace new beginnings with new experiences. With prayer, determination, and the "7 Keys to Letting Go" process, I found freedom from the traumas of yesteryear.

Whether it is the death of a loved one, domestic violence, a broken relationship, or sexual abuse, individuals hold on to hurts, reliving the pain over and over. Releasing yourself from emotional trauma is crucial because living in the past prevents you from living in the present. Your present is the only place you can experience new beginnings. To prepare and receive newness into your life, you must first remove the old. But if your heart is occupied with the past, how is there any room for the present?

Letting go of yesteryear is not easy, but you owe it to yourself to release the bondage and embrace the process of healing and freedom. The first step to releasing is to both **recognize** and acknowledge your pain. Pretending it's not there or trying to rationalize your feelings away only keeps you in emotional bondage. However, recognizing your hurt can be the difference between healing or staying in a state of pain. You must bring your feelings into your conscious thoughts so that you can deal with them and begin the healing process.

In Romans 12:2, it says, "Do not conform to the patterns of this world but be transformed by the renewing of your mind. Then you will be able to test and approve what God's will is, his good, pleasing and perfect will." When you acknowledge your emotional pain, you are no longer conforming to the thoughts and the experiences of the past. Instead, you are working to transform and to renew your mind so that you can embrace the present. This healing process takes a changed mindset in conjunction with prayer and perseverance.

Once you recognize that your past is keeping you from living in the present, you must make a conscious commitment to let go and to work through the healing process. You must commit to letting go of the past and to looking at it from a different perspective. You must recognize what your past did to you and you must approach it differently. You have to ask yourself what you learned from the experience and how you can use what you went through to help others.

Proverbs 4:25-26 says, "Let your eyes look straight ahead; fix your gaze directly before you. Give careful thought to the paths for your feet and be steadfast in all your ways." After you have committed to releasing the trauma, you should begin looking straight ahead. You should be done with looking back at your past, your gaze must be fixed directly before you. Your commitment to your healing is what plants your feet steadfastly while your prayers, the process, and your perseverance will assist in keeping you committed. Your healing begins with a plan, with a purpose, and with an expectation to release the trauma of yesteryear!

You must now **label** your emotions to describe and identify how you feel. Labeling your emotions is the first step in dealing with them effectively.

Often, the most obvious label is not the most accurate one. We all experience three basic emotions: love, anger, and fear which are like the primary colors, red, yellow, and blue. Just as every color is one of these colors, the same is true that every feeling is connected to either love, anger, or fear. Because emotions are not always manifested as what they really are, you must listen to each one to test whether the information is accurate.

Even when your emotions do not match your situation, they are communicating information. For example, feelings of guilt might indicate you need to set boundaries for yourself. Unnecessary feelings of fear may indicate that you need to challenge yourself in a specific area. Becoming aware of your emotions helps you to decide whether they fit the facts of your situation. When labeling your emotions, it is best to have two words to describe how you are feeling. You will be surprised at the depth of your emotions and the deeper ones hidden under the obvious ones. Labeling your emotions helps you to understand them, to control them, and to make more informed decisions.

Proverbs 17:22 says, "A cheerful heart is good medicine, but a crushed spirit dries up the bones."

When you label and identify how your past affects your emotions, you begin to understand them, and your heart begins to change. In doing so, you can manage your emotions, and they begin to work for you rather than against you.

After labeling and identifying your emotions, it is now time to **express** your hurt. You must express how the hurt makes you feel, either to the person that hurt you or through one of three recommended sources: therapy, journaling, or reflecting.

Expressing those identified emotions helps you understand what the hurt is about. When expressing your hurt, it is best to use the "I" feelings. Using the "I" word helps to describe the extent of your emotions, i.e. anger, sadness, fear, etc. and it shows that you are taking responsibility for you, your emotions, and your healing.

Expressing your hurt also means that you are open to recognizing how you are feeling or that you are open to controlling your pain. When you numb sadness, you also numb happiness. Withholding emotions causes you to not only suppress the bad feelings, but also the good ones. In other words, it is important to pay attention to your emotions, to identify them and to express them. When you withhold feelings, they can cause serious mental or physical problems. However, while expressing, you must remember to be responsible with when, how, and where you express them. Careful expression must be in a healthy environment accompanied by coping strategies.

Ephesians 4:18 says, "They are darkened in their understanding and separated from the life of God because of the ignorance that is in them due to the hardening of their hearts."

According to BibleRef (2002-2020), Paul notes the difference between a life wallowing under the power of sin, or in this case, a life stuck in the past and not moving forward as opposed to a life thriving in the power of Christ. The people of God are called to "put away" the things which entangle us. This includes malice, slander, commotion, and bitterness, anger, fear, sadness, and anything that keeps us from living in the fullness of God.

Throughout the process of releasing the trauma of yesteryear, you learned that your emotions keep you stuck in the past and prevents you from moving forward. You recognized the effects of your emotions, committed to releasing the past, identified your emotions, and took responsibility by expressing those feelings. Now, let's talk about how to control those emotions.

When you become **aware** (gain knowledge and realization) of how your emotions are connected to your past, it helps you to not only understand them, but also to manage them. Often you hear people say, "I can't control my emotions." This is not true, because once you become aware of your thinking, you learn to control your emotions.

Let us discuss how to control your emotions by focusing on your thinking. After expressing your emotions and how the experience made you feel, you can begin directing your emotions rather than allowing them to direct you. While the painful experiences may trigger unpleasant feelings and reactions, they do not cause them. Most of what you tell yourself is controlled by your subconscious which derives from the beliefs you have at any given time.

When you manage what you think and don't allow your emotions to do so, you oversee your behaviors and determine how the events in your life unfold. Your awareness of your emotions helps to transform your thoughts.

For example, your IQ can help you get into an ivy league school. However, it is your ability to recognize your emotions and how they affect your thoughts and behaviors that help you to manage your emotions and stress levels while taking the test to get into that ivy league school.

You must be aware of what you tell yourself so that you can direct emotions rather than having your emotions directing your choices. Directing your emotions regulates the triggers from the past and controls your behaviors and the events that unfold in your life. Remember, you are the only person in charge of your emotional responses, thoughts, and actions. It is only you who can protect your peace of mind regardless of your past or present experiences.

The more you become aware of your emotions, the more you realize that you have the power to control your emotional states. You understand the connection between your words, your thoughts, and your emotions. By making small changes in your thoughts, you let go of the past and choose how you experience future events.

Proverbs 20:5 says, "The purposes of a person's heart are deep waters, but one who has insight draws them out." Recognizing how your emotions affect you, making a commitment to change, identifying, and expressing them, and developing awareness are the keys to understanding and controlling your thoughts."

True strength is not physical, but rather lies in the ability to influence and control your thoughts and emotions. Your emotions are the driving force for your behaviors because the decisions you choose are based on how you feel. Once you take control of your thoughts, you make decisions from a place of control.

The final step of releasing the trauma of yesteryear is to **evict** unforgiveness. When you hold on to past hurts, it intensifies your emotions and keeps them alive. Alexander Pope said, "To err is human, but to forgive is divine." You may feel justified or even vindicated in holding on to unforgiveness, but it keeps you attached to the past. Forgiveness does not erase the experience, instead looks at that experience with a different perspective.

We are challenged and our worthiness is called into question when we are hurt, especially by our loved ones. Our brain works to defend us from future hurt and through our thoughts and emotions we hold on to sadness, anger, fear, etc. to keep the pain alive.

Paul Boese said, "Forgiveness doesn't change the past, but it enlarges the future." The more you become aware of your emotions, the easier it becomes to forgive. You understand that the emotions from the past are a call for self-love and appreciation, and forgiveness is the key. Not only do you forgive those that hurt you, but you also forgive yourself for holding on to anger, fear, and any other negative emotion. In becoming aware of your emotions, you heal and move to inner freedom. If you hold on to the past, you stay connected to the person that hurt you and that keeps the poisonous feelings alive. All those feelings attached to the past are like a poison slowly killing you emotionally and possibly physically through depression, stress, etc. Evicting the emotions and forgiving those who hurt you shows that you no longer allow their behavior to cause you pain.

2 Corinthians 5:17 says, "Therefore, if anyone is in Christ, the new creation has come; the old has gone, the new is here."

Forgiveness comes from a deep faith that you are enough, that love is abundant, and that even though you were wronged, you do not have to experience the hurt of trying to have that debt paid back to you. As a new creation in Christ, you have the control to let go of what is not important and to make room for what matters.

For everyone, including praying wives in waiting, before you can move on to marriage or to any other place in life, you must first work through and let go of past hurts. Once you do, you will then be free to move forward with your life without regret, bitterness, or resentment.

Visit audreybrooks.org to take the *Release the Trauma of YesterYear* assessment.

Prayer: Releasing the Trauma of Yesteryear

Father God, we thank you for releasing us from the trauma of yesteryear. In 2 Corinthians 5:15, it states, "Therefore, if any man be in Christ, he is a new creature: old things are passed away; behold, all things have become new." Father God, we are released from the stronghold of the hurt and pain and we now walk in freedom. We are no longer victims of our past but we are victorious in You. Therefore, we have forgotten the former things and our thoughts no longer dwell in the past.

You are doing a new thing in us and we thank you that we are not defined by our past, but instead, our past has made us stronger. We thank you that all bitterness, wrath, malice, and unforgiveness no longer resides in us, but rather the spirit of love, peace, joy, patience, kindness, and self-control lives in us.

Father, we choose to fully trust You with all our heart and lean not to our own understanding. We acknowledge your ways for us, Lord, because we know You will make our paths straight. We will continue to work to fulfill the purpose for which You have Ordained us. We will remain focused on the Truth of what lies ahead of us, for the righteous shall move onward and forward and those with pure hearts shall become stronger and stronger. We have a new purpose and we will reach the end of the race and receive the prize, for we know that all things work together for good for those who love God, who are called according to his purpose.

We pray this in the most powerful name of our Lord Jesus Christ, who guards our paths of justice and watches over the ways of His saints.

Amen.

Marriage + Ministry
Serving God's People Together

Debra Pope Reddick

Introduction

No one ever told me what to expect when you marry a man of God nor did anyone inform me that marriage is really ministry. That very ministry began for me in 2001 when I was single, saved, and sanctified. I had no idea that I was in ministry until one day when I was at a meeting with a group of single women having bible study and discussing our life challenges.

Later, there I was preaching and teaching in churches and venues throughout Florida and Georgia, wondering when and how I'd gotten there. I realized that God really does have a sense of humor because everything seemed to happen so fast before I completely realized what was going on. However, when I look back on things, I can clearly see that God was always showing up in my life when I didn't know it and sometimes even when I didn't want Him to.

At the age of twenty-one, I entered into a five year marriage. The day of our ceremony, before the vows were spoken, I knew that this marriage was not a part of God's plan for my life. However, I proceeded with the ceremony because I didn't know how to get out of it. Needless to say, we ended up divorcing. Years after divorcing my first husband, I knew that one day I would get married again however, while I was single, I never seemed to date the right man. I didn't consult God regarding my relationships because I never even knew I was supposed to. There were times that I was willing to compromise and settle, but ladies, isn't that what many of us do? We settle and ask God to cosign on what we want, but don't ask Him what He has for us?

I was so busy doing God's work that I didn't have time to think of dating or marriage. In 2005, I received an assignment from God to relocate to

Atlanta. I didn't have the money, a job, or a place to live, however, God opened a door for me to live in a brand-new home rent free. Nobody but God! Living in Atlanta proved to be an assignment that I didn't entirely understand or truly appreciated. All I knew was that I'd been sent there by God and that it must have been for a reason. However, after approximately nine months, I was released to move back to Tampa. What? I'd moved everything I owned to Atlanta and now God was sending me back to Tampa. It didn't make any sense to me, but I was obedient. While living in Atlanta my life was a time of isolation and consecration, focused on God, prayer, and His assignment for me. It is was years later that God reveal His reason for sending me to Atlanta.

In November 2006, less than a month after I relocated back to Florida, I was offered a job that I was able to start immediately. In April 2007 while at my job, my sister in law met a co-worker in her area that she wanted me to meet and she had begun calling him her brother in law. I used to ask her why are you doing that I'm not looking for a husband. She said she believed that was going to be her brother in law. I didn't meet up with him until weeks later, but when I did, I noticed that he was a nice, handsome, well dressed charismatic man. However, I wasn't looking for a relationship, neither was I prepared for one. He and I became friends, so I decided that I wanted some of the women that were in my group to meet him. However, it never seemed to happen. He told me one day that he liked me, and I gave him such a look that he felt like he had put his foot in his mouth. I was caught off guard and didn't know what to say, so I said nothing. One day I heard the spirit of the Lord say to me, "How dare you give away something that I'm giving you." I felt really small!

I believe the story of Ruth was alive and manifesting in my life. I was busy and focused on my assignment, so much so that I didn't even try to put my head up for a moment. I had tunnel vision. My life was dedicated to the things of God, dedicated to teaching single women how to live holy while single and being kept by God. In this group we were each other's' accountability partners and were available whenever there was a need. Few of the women were married which was a blessing to help in this assignment. As a single woman, I was kept by God and celibate for seven years. Yes, seven years is a long time and many ask the question of how. How are you doing it? Sex and intimacy with a man was not my focus! As a saved, single woman, you should be more concerned about doing the work of the kingdom than worrying and wondering about who your husband is, when will he show up or whether or not you will ever marry.

Marriage is more than saying I do

Marriage is more than saying I do, especially when you marry someone with a call on their life. Knowing that marriage is ministry and accepting the assignment to stand alongside my husband as his help mate has been a calling that I've taken seriously. Making a decision to marry should be more than the day of the wedding. Many times people spend so much time and energy planning the wedding and less time planning the marriage. The wedding is only one day, marriage is supposed to be for a lifetime.

We know that God has a purpose for each of us, and we should understand that knowing the purpose of your marriage helps to shape the direction in which your life should go. Getting married for the wrong reasons can lead you down a path of destruction. Don't enter marriage because you just want a husband, want "legal" sex, or because you're just lonely. Remember, marriage is more than the wedding day. When that wedding day is over and reality sets in, you'll find that marriage takes patience, it takes work, and you must be willing to sacrifice to make it a success at any cost.

I remember the day we got married. It was August 2009, I was a beautiful bride and my soon to be husband look ever so handsome. The wedding and reception was awesome. Everything was planned and went off perfectly. We were in love and ready to start our marriage the right way. Of course, I was marrying a man of God and I was excited to share my life and love again.

I had to learn that although the two of us became one when we got married, we were still individuals with different personalities. I had been independent for a very long time. Throughout my entire adult life I'd been single longer than my two combined marriages, so when I got married, I still had the mindset that I should still be able to do what I wanted to and he couldn't tell me certain things and that I could take care of myself. My God, that was such the wrong attitude to have. I used to throw the words, "I'm independent" around like it was water, until one day I heard a friend preach. In her sermon she admitted to saying the same thing. She also stated that God had convicted her and told her that she'd had a spirit of pride. That hit me like a ton of bricks. I knew at that time God was speaking to me. Was I operating in pride in my marriage? Indeed, I was, and I quickly realized that the word "I" was big in my vocabulary. I had to repent immediately.

My husband wasn't in ministry, but I was. He said that he didn't want to be in ministry, yet he was willing to support whatever God had planned for my life. Well, it turns out that my husband's plans were truly not what God had planned.

When God called my husband to pastor, he was in the shower and the Holy Spirit came upon him and saturated him with His presence. He immediately got out the shower to tell me what was going on. After he opened his mouth to tell me what the Holy Spirit was saying, I immediately knew that it indeed was God speaking. I took hours of dictation with instructions from God on how He wanted us to start a church. That night our lives totally transformed, and marriage and ministry truly began.

My responsibility as a wife was and is to make sure that the vision that God has placed in my husband goes forth. Women of God, we are the help mates that God has designed just for a particular man of God. There are women who want to be married to a pastor, but what I will tell you when you marry a pastor you marry ministry. If God has called you to be a pastor's wife, He will equip you. This is a responsibility that should not be taken lightly. This is an important office. As pastor's wives, you must be confident in who you are, and you should not depend on others to validate you. You must be able to trust your husband's assignment because he has to be available for the people you both serve.

In ministry, there will be challenges, setbacks, oppositions, as well as triumphs. When serving God's people, you will develop endurance while long suffering. In these nine years of ministry, we've had to make sacrifices for the good of the ministry. There have been times when we've wanted to quit, however, we trusted God. Being a Pastor or a Co-Pastor is not a job, it's a commitment to the call of God. The word of God tells us that many are called and few are chosen. You must be strong in the Lord, truly understanding that the assignment you've been given by God is a covenant that you've made with Him. Quitting on God is not an option.

Part of what keeps us going is that we are each other's confidantes and we trust each other, not only in our marriage but also in ministry. Throughout the years, in serving God together in ministry, we've grown and we understand that serving God and His people is what we were called to do even before God brought us together.

Ministry of the "Holy Hush"

Most of the time women think we are an expert on any subject, but we're not. Sometimes, I think we just like to hear ourselves speak. Our husbands let us talk at times, but I had to learn that there is a time and a place to be quiet. Being able to keep our mouths closed is truly a gift for some women. As a woman of God in ministry with my husband, I had to learn the art of the ministry of the "Holy Hush". Holy hush you say, what is that? I'm glad you ask. I tell you that it's learning how to keep my mouth closed. Women we're not experts on every subject, we don't have to have the last word, and not everything we say is gospel.

Being married and serving in ministry alongside the man of God doesn't mean that you will not still have disagreements and arguments. The enemy attacks us even more than those that are not serving God or serving in ministry. Throughout these last eleven years of marriage, there have been times when we both felt like we wanted to throw in the towel in our marriage. How can that be? Well, there's pressure in marriage and in ministry. We are serving God, working in ministry to help expand the Kingdom of God, yet it seems like every time we turned around, something is happening and often times it's not favorable. All of these things combined causes life to become challenging and overwhelming and it seems so simple, to just throw in the towel.

Words of Encouragement

While you're single, allow yourself to be committed to God and to what He would have you to do during your season of singleness. You will make mistakes during that time and there will be things you don't understand but it's okay. We learn from our mistakes. You are not perfect and God isn't expecting you to be.

Earlier in the chapter, I told you that there was a reason why God sent me to Atlanta and He revealed it to me years later. Well, what God revealed was while I was in my season of Isolation and Consecration in Atlanta he was preparing me and my future husband. At that time, he didn't live in Tampa nor was he spiritually prepared. As for me, God needed me to be strengthen in my prayer life as well making sure I wasn't going to be distracted for what would be my next assignment which was marriage and ministry. Many times you don't know what the plans that God has for you however just stay focus on Him. Trust God and trust the process!

As Ruth was busy on her assignment in the field, she was focused on that. When Boaz noticed her, she was still committed to the work that she was doing. That is the same dedication to God you should have. If you believe God has someone for you, when that time comes, He will present you. You don't have to chase marriage or ministry. If you are to be married, then you're already a wife. The scripture tells us in Proverbs 18:22, *He who finds a wife finds a good thing, And obtains favor from the LORD.* Prepare yourself for the journey by submitting and committing yourself to God. Allow Him to lead you and to teach you how to be a wife.

If you're blessed to serve God's people together with your husband, support him, serve him, encourage him, love him and most of all always pray for him. Be his intercessor. Understand that God trust you with each other and He trust you with His people. It's a privilege and an honor to be chosen by God for such a calling as this. Don't ever take your assignment nor your calling for granted.

Prayer

Heavenly Father, I pray for the woman of God that's waiting on the man of God that you have ordained just for her. I pray that she will develop patience and endurance. I pray that she won't get in a hurry and settle or compromise for whomever comes her way. Instead, I pray that she's strong enough to wait on You. And Heavenly Father, when she's praying and can't hear You, allow her not to get discouraged, but to hold on to her faith in You. Heavenly Father, while she's waiting patiently as a single woman, keep her and strengthen her for the assignment of marriage and ministry. I pray that if You have called her to ministry while she's married, that she is able to trust the process and allow her to be led by her husband, her priest. Bless the marriage and all that they may encounter in ministry. May *You* always be there ultimate focus. This is my prayer, in Jesus name, Amen.

The Kids Are Grown and Gone, *Now What?*

Maryann Rivera-Dannert

I was sitting on the couch reading a magazine, when I looked over at James and said: "Oh, my gosh! It's just us, now what?"
Bewildered, he looked at me and said, "What did you say?"
I repeated myself.

As I write this, it's been exactly six months since we've become empty nesters. My youngest decided to move out, and out of the blue I find myself struggling with the fact that the kids are gone. Now what? What exactly am I supposed to do?

I'm having feelings of doubt, feelings of uncertainty, and a sense of mistaken identity. There are no children to hide behind, no one stealing time away from my need to pay attention to my husband. My husband, you know, that man that after twelve years of marriage still squeezes the toothpaste from the middle of the tube or puts the toilet paper roll on the wrong way. When the children are grown and gone, you start to notice the little things about your spouse that you never had time to deal with before.

Let's go back to the beginning for a little content, shall we?

One crazy evening in January of 2008, boy stumbles across girl's MySpace page. Boy contacts girl, she smiles and they commence to have an online conversation. A few weeks later, boy asks girl to dinner. She says yes. Three months later, boy proposes, they get married four months after that. *The end.*

That was really just the beginning. Getting to the point of saying, "I do" was a journey all on its own. Friendships were lost, there was a temporary move in with the parents, as an ex packed their stuff and exited the premises. Oh yeah, and we eloped! We literally started our marriage kind of backwards.

With so many disappointments up until that point, we decided to sit down and have a heart to heart. I remember asking James what he thought was the most important thing in planning the wedding. He said, "That we end up husband and wife." This would be both of our second marriages, and while we had done it before, being mature adults now, we were getting married for love and we wanted to show everyone. As a result, we ended up scrapping all the plans, contacted the pastor and our best friends, met at the beach, and exchanged our vows. Bystanders thought we were practicing until they saw the ring exchange, the kiss and the hugs.

Our wedding ceremony took place on a Friday evening followed by our engagement party Saturday afternoon, and then my bachelorette party Saturday night. I told you we started things kind of backwards.

I wish that I could say we've lived happily ever after since that moment, but this isn't a fairy tale. Its real life, with real people and these real people have a real past. Both James and I have been married before. In fact, when I met him, although separated for almost a decade, he was still married. Once before, I had dated a guy that was married but legally separated. I was not going down that road again and I made that very clear to him. If we were going to pursue a serious relationship, he needed to get a divorce. Consequently, I connected him with a divorce attorney and when he proceeded to go through with the divorce, I knew he was serious. That, and the fact that he continued to pursue me. As for me, because I had just ended a toxic and unhealthy relationship, I realized that I had a lot of work of my own to do, a great deal of internal work.

When my last relationship ended, I made the decision that going forward I would not settle, nor would I sacrifice my desires or needs, for anyone. My attitude was that it was either my way or the highway. I was not going to put anyone else's dreams, goals, or interests before mine. I was going to be vocal and let my demands be known. Not only would my demands be heard, they would be taken seriously. I was not the same person I'd been before as I went into that new relationship with James.

We got married fast. He said he knew from the moment he met me that we'd end up getting married. I was honest with him years ago when, during marriage counseling, I revealed that I married him out of religious obligation. I didn't want to live in sin as I'd just started going back to church and had recommitted myself to Christ. To some, that may sound harsh, but it's the truth. The one thing we told each other years ago was that we would always be honest and not attempt to protect the other's feelings by sugar-coating how we were feeling. We would be honest and allow the other individual to feel how they wanted and needed to feel.

Separately, we have a total of six children, but we have no children together. We'd both known that the day would arrive when my youngest would leave the nest, we just didn't anticipate it would happen as early as it did. We were caught off guard and I was not prepared. As soon as my youngest moved out, I found myself thinking, that this was it. It was just us, and I truly believed we're definitely going to get a divorce.

A quick Google search will show you that an estimated sixty percent of second marriages end in divorce. That number is higher for empty nesters. As I started having feelings of doubt and uncertainty, feelings of mistaken identity also started to creep up. Without the kids in the house to occupy my time and keep me from thinking too deeply about myself, I started to wonder who I was, how I fit into the marriage, and what was about to happen now. As a result, we had one of our talks and during that talk, we laid it all out on the table. We'd been there before, but this time felt different. This particular time we realized that it was just us, we didn't have the kids to use as an excuse to, or not to, do anything. We couldn't hold on to our marriage for the kid's sake, or for financial reasons. We had to hold on for us.

It was during this talk that we became conscious of the fact that the rules we had played by before no longer applied. The dynamics of our relationship had changed. We now had to be intentional. We each asked the other what they needed from the marriage. He needed respect and validation, I needed intimacy and security. It was at that moment that I made the decision to stop bringing up divorce, that was not an option for us. Divorce would not be an option for us because we both knew what we needed and wanted from each other and from the marriage. Furthermore, we were both committed to making it work. When I tell you that I am married to the most understanding, kind, levelheaded, and supportive man on the planet, I really am. More than that, he gets me. He understands my moments of self-doubt and he does not judge me, he never has. It had taken nearly twelve years for me to see that God had given me the person I needed with a few sprinkles of what I wanted on the side.

Up to that moment, several things occurred that led to a new realization for me. For starters, my husband was receptive to counseling. Men are sometimes reluctant to seek counseling, especially black men. There is a stigma about opening up and speaking about your feelings. But the fact that he was open minded about it was one of the first signs. Then there was the talk we had shortly after my youngest moved out. While we'd had numerous conversations over the years, this talk was truly transformative for us both. We were partners and we recognized that our Daddy in Heaven always knows what we need, and He never lets us down.

Since my daughter left home, it has been just us. We've made a decision and a commitment to each other and our marriage, to reconnect in purposeful ways. There's no magic wand, it's a choice and it's one that must be renewed daily. We've made joint goals in addition to our individual goals. We have to know where we are headed and therefore, we must plan. I love to relax and unwind with a good book and he prefers to play video games. Those are our individual pleasures, yet, when we come together we love to cuddle up on the couch and watch some of our favorite shows. Even in a marriage, it's important to remain individuals, however, when it's just the two, spending time together to connect is critical.

Sitting back as I admire my husband from across the room, I've crafted five tips on how to reconnect with your spouse during the empty nesters season of one's marriage. The tips, with a brief summary are as follows:

1. *Have fun:* Life stops for no one. We cannot allow our children, jobs, friends or family, to consume our time or energy. Having fun with one another keeps us laughing. It increases serotonin and endorphins, the feel-good chemicals in our brains and body. After all, it's just the two of you now, you have to fight to keep the flame burning.

2. *Invest in your marriage:* Over our twelve years of marriage we have attended three marriage retreats. We've walked away from each retreat with so many nuggets of wisdom and the connection we now have to

each other is indescribable. I highly recommend A Weekend to Remember and the WinShape Retreat.

3. *Communicate:* We want to think and believe that our spouses should be able to read our minds and automatically know what we want and need. They can't. We have to open up and discuss what is troubling us. We ought to be able to express ourselves and talk about our interests, desires, hopes, goals, and dreams. How does your partner fit into your aspirations? There are two of you in the marriage, it'll take both of you collectively working together to make it work. I also don't believe in the saying about not going to bed angry. Sometimes, walking away is the best option in the moment. Let your partner know that you are not in a place to continue the conversation; that you need some time to gather your thoughts and maturely continue the conversation at an agreed upon time. Remember, once something negative is said, you cannot take it back.

4. *Be You:* My belief is that the bible verse in Genesis 2:24: "Therefore a man shall leave his father and his mother and hold fast to his wife, and they shall become one flesh", is misunderstood by some. It is important to have shared interests and goals, etc., but you do not have to do everything together and you certainly do not have to like the exact same things. It is healthy to have your own goals and interests. Yes, you are married, but you are still you.

5. *Pray:* James and I have the same religious beliefs. We believe in the Father, the Son, and the Holy Spirit, the Holy Trinity. However, we don't go to church. We read our bibles, our devotionals, and we definitely pray. We pray for our friends, family, jobs, politicians, the world as a whole, and we keep each other covered in prayer. That is the glue that binds and holds us together.

My hope and desire is that the tips above, when implemented, will bring you and your spouse closer to one another. My suggestions are from a personal and professional point of view. As a wife of twelve years, I am also a Certified Life Coach, known as The Fearless Living Coach. My life's mission is to inspire, empower, and equip women from coast to coast to live the life they've always desired. A fearless life! So, what exactly does *fearless* mean? It means being free to live our lives by the standards that we set for ourselves based on our *truths, talents, and strengths*, not by the words, thoughts, or actions of others. It means to boldly declare that the limiting beliefs instilled in us are not us! We courageously affirm that we are crushing those lies and we are going to live the life we've always dreamed and desired. We commit to **Fearless & Fabulous Living!**

I invite you to visit my website at **maryannriveradannert.com.** Please sign up to claim your free guides:

1. *The Whys of Goals.*
2. *Guide to Fabulousness.*
3. *50 Ways to Connect with You.*

In closing, I leave you with one of my favorite quotes:
What lies behind us and what lies before us are tiny matters compared to what lies within us.
Ralph Waldo Emerson

Will the Real Denise Please Stand Up?

M. Denise Simmons

I was a slut bucket!

Yes, I said it! I *was* a slut bucket back in my day. Today, my single friends frustrate me when they say, "You don't understand, you're married." But if they only knew what I went through to get to where I am today – 11 years later married to my King, Mario Simmons!

In order for you to understand my story, the things I will suggest to you, and some strategies you can apply, I have to start on the day I lost my virginity to my high school sweetheart while I was attending college at the University of Florida. I was about eighteen or nineteen and I'd decided that I was ready to engage in sexual intercourse. I came to this conclusion because things in college was becoming very tempting and very dangerous for me. However, I knew that my first time needed to be with someone special, with someone I knew, and with someone who loved me.

I thought that before I opened my legs to that hot fraternity guy or to any old "Joe Schmo", I wanted to at least "give it up" to someone who cared about me deeply. So, I did it, and after that, things were never the same for me sexually. I became fast and very promiscuous, but you wouldn't have ever known that because I wasn't boisterous about it all and because I rarely shared my business. Only extremely close friends knew the real Denise.

I didn't know it at the time, but I was obviously going through something deeply rooted. I would find myself having one night stands, or dealing with guys who were in relationships, or dating men nearly twenty years my senior. Or even worse, I was dating and having sex with two guys at the same time. And on top of that, I had a curable STD and had to make that embarrassing phone calls to all the men I'd been involved with so that they could get tested.

What topped it off for me, however, was that while I was living in New York, I was dealing with a dude I'd met during a college road trip with my line sisters. I thought this man was my husband. I met his family and they loved me. He served in ministry and that was a huge plus for me. I didn't even mind that he had a son, I was in love with this dude! I saw a future with him.

The last time he came to visit me in New York and we had sex, it was unprotected. When he left, I was terrified because I was alone. In fact, I immediately felt "alone" because after telling him that I was pregnant, he advised me to take the Plan B pill. That was my wakeup call! I was disgusted with myself, I felt embarrassed, but most of all I was hurting deep inside because I was yearning to be in a committed relation and to be loved in a special way. But I didn't get that. Instead, what I got was the realization that I ended up sacrificing too much of myself. I would pay for airfare, I would make all the accommodations for us to do things together. I came to the understanding that I wasn't being put on a pedestal by the men I was dating. I was giving up too much of myself way too fast and was expecting the world in return. It didn't work out that way!

A Praying Wife in Waiting

That realization hit me hard, so much so that I had a true and intentional "Come to Jesus moment." I was tired of giving it up with no real commitment, I was done with just having a relationship centered around sex and nothing else, and I was over the fact that I'd had more sexual partners then I had fingers! I remember praying fervently and crying out to God about where I was currently in life and about how I just wanted to be in a committed relationship with a man who loved me and was serious about being in that relationship with me.

So, I prayed and fasted for about a month. And within that month I had a dream that I was walking down the aisle in a wedding dress toward this tall, dark, and handsome man and *I was happy*! I think it was about a week later that I met my husband, Mario, and eleven years later we are still happily married. I love that man with all of my heart!

Now here is the kicker, for the past three years I have been an entrepreneur and that has been no easy ordeal, especially in a marriage. At certain points in our marriage, my pursuit of entrepreneurship has tested us greatly, but because of what I went through in the past and the kind of man my husband is, we always got through it. Why?

Because we kept God in the midst of it all, truly! He was the only one that got us up from those downs.

So, I say to you, be honest with yourself and with where you are so that God can reveal to you where He wants to take you. With every major thing I ever desired in life, I had an awakening moment where I was honest and real about what was really happening. I couldn't live in denial and expect mountains to move on my behalf and I couldn't have expectations of greatness while not even preparing myself mentally for it. It doesn't work like that.

So, I leave you with this one important strategy; in order to be real with yourself and to know what you want, spend time with yourself in God. Whether that is through prayer, fasting, going to church, reading scripture, etc., just allow your thoughts to be filtered through what God is saying about you. But you *have* to spend some time with Him!

Encouraging scripture: Do not be anxious about anything, but in every situation, by prayer and petition, with thanksgiving, present your requests to God. And the peace of God, which transcends all understanding, will guard your hearts and your minds in Christ Jesus. **- Philippians 4:6-7**

Balancing Acts:
Strategies on Finding Balance in Your Marriage

Sierra Hilaire

As a woman, wife, mother and entrepreneur, the most challenging thing that I've faced is being able to balance it all and take care of myself in the midst. My husband and I have been married for fifteen years and together we have four amazing children. We started our family very young, when I was only fifteen years old. Growing up without the right guidance and family support, I wasn't as fortunate to have a healthy family and marriage modeled before me. So, what happens then? You usually do what you were taught, saw or experienced, right?

Although my heart was in the right place and I wanted to have a perfect family and a perfect marriage, the fear of my past had me in bondage because it taught me that there was no such thing as perfect. I had witnessed my parents get a divorce after an affair. As a result, it left my mother, me, and my sisters broken. Not knowing that I had carried that pain around with me all of those years, just like in the story of Job, what I feared came upon me.

In 2016, God called me to launch a family conference called "The Freedom Experience" that would literally change my life forever. For the first time I was free, my heart was transformed, and life began to get better. From there my business and my family continued to grow and more opportunities and responsibilities were presented to me. Not having much knowledge about successfully managing a ministry, I quickly became overwhelmed, stressed, and sick. I wasn't spending time with God in prayer, in the word, and in worship like I needed to. My body was in so much pain on some days that I could barely exercise as a means of getting the stamina or the strength needed to keep up. My marriage was being neglected because the little bit of energy I did have went on the kids, the housework, and the business tasks.

With me not realizing how this stretching of myself was impacting my husband, we continued on with our normal routine until that night in March that changed everything. While my husband and I slept, the Holy Spirit woke me up at about three a.m. Suddenly, I had this deep gut feeling that something was terribly wrong. I turned over to my husband and surprisingly, he was awake as well. I lay there for a minute, gripped with the fear of hearing bad news that I knew was to come. Somehow, I'd gained the courage to ask him, "Do you have something that you want to talk to me about"? It was then that my husband shared with me what no wife wants to hear. He'd had an affair earlier that year and he'd done it at the time that I was going through my phase of being overwhelmed, stressed, and sick. He explained that he'd felt powerless, like he couldn't help me, and that the guilt was eating away at him on the inside. As my husband spoke, I remember trembling and sweating so badly, it was as if someone had just electrocuted me.

It was in that moment that what I like to call my "Window of Grace" overshadowed our bed and I heard the Lord say to me that if I didn't forgive him right now, I would never be able to do it. I immediately told my husband that I forgive him without him even asking for my forgiveness first. My heart was so broken, but I felt so whole. As we laid in bed crying and embracing one another, God instantly restored my marriage and my health. For the first time in a long time I felt so connected, so vulnerable, and so unafraid to be who I really was in front of my husband. From there, I learned that we were in that situation because we had stopped making God and each other a priority, and because we needed to deal with some unresolved issues from our past.

For an entire year, my husband and I spent much time getting to know each other all over again because the people we were now weren't the same people we'd been before everything happened. We took long walks together and talked for hours about things that happened in our childhood. Our conversations were on a much deeper level because our intimacy had been restored, so we were unafraid of truly expressing how we felt and we knew we could do it without being judged. Making time for each other was easier than it had ever been as our priorities had shifted. No matter what was going on with our children or in ministry, we didn't allow anything to get between us in the new space of love that we'd discovered.

Sierra Hilaire: Married 15 Years

Although our relationship was growing stronger and healthier, the warfare had intensified. Emotionally, I was still processing everything that had happened. I found myself needing to get in a quiet space daily to cry out to God for understanding, strength, and wisdom. My marriage was working, but my soul was struggling. I knew that my prayer life had to go to another level if we were going to really survive the storm. 1st Peter 5:8 says, "Be well balanced and always alert, because your enemy, the devil, roams around incessantly, like a roaring lion looking for its prey to devour". I had to be intentional with everything, with planning, date nights, dinner time, household chores, clients etc. I was trying to keep myself together while God healed me from that traumatic experience, and that was going to take some time.

I remember our neighbor's cousin moving in with them during that time in my marriage, and for whatever reason that dude began making passes at me on what seemed liked every day. So, on top of what I was currently dealing with, I now had another issue to contend with. I would speak when I saw the neighbor's cousin, but beyond that, I kept it moving.

As I went into my evening counseling sessions with God, one day He revealed to me that I needed to not take what was going on lightly. He said, "Anytime someone hurts you, the enemy will always create opportunities for you to pay them back." That's exactly what could have happened if I would have entertained the neighbor or allowed my emotions to be unstable and lead me to play the victim role. That revelation changed my whole perspective because it made sense. I understood that I had been doing that all along. When my husband and I would have a disagreement, I would spitefully withhold sex because I thought that was how I could get my way, how I could control the situation, or how I could pay him back. It was a vicious cycle that

was showing up in my life and it was impacting my marriage, my faith and my health. God could not allow me to keep moving forward in that condition, not if He was going to get the glory out of my life and ministry.

He allowed that breakdown in my marriage to be used as a breakthrough to bring about true balance and healing for both myself and my husband. My relationship with God grew beyond what I could imagine and in the process I started to see that every

Sierra Hilaire: Married 15 Years

time life got busy and I stopped spending time with Him, there would be a shift in my relationship with my husband. So, I began to use the lesson as a tool to check the temperature of my self-care and my marriage.

Shortly after the Lord revealed what was going on with our neighbor, He blessed us with a new home that we closed on in less than thirty days. The scripture says in 1st Corinthians 10:13, "No temptation has overtaken or enticed you that is not common to human experience; but God is faithful, and He will not let you be tempted beyond your ability, but along with the temptation, He will provide the way of escape, so that you will be able to endure it." I knew that if we didn't get out of that environment, things would not have ended well.

When we finally did move, I realized that being in a different space was actually helping me grow through the process. It also sparked new emotions of excitement, joy, and gratitude. Managing your emotions is a huge deal after you've experienced any traumatic thing. The highs and lows are real, but with the right approach, open communication and a decision to never allow yourself to go back to how

Sierra Hilaire: Married 15 Years

things used to be will be key in the restoration process.

As women, it's so important that we make our self-care a priority. Some of the ways we can do that is by making sure we are staying connected to our spiritual source, by eating a balanced diet, and by taking the right supplements to compensate for our nutritional deficiencies. We should also get in some exercise, spend some quiet time alone, be around people, and listen to things that feed our soul. And most importantly, we should operate in our divine purpose. My marriage is a part of my purpose, so making it a priority is not only the right thing to do, it also pleases God.

He doesn't want us out in the streets saving the world like Superwoman while behind closed doors things are falling apart. When the world sees us getting divorced, living dysfunctional lives, and living with all of the chaos that results from not being able to let go and forgive, or simply not having our homes and lives in order, that is how Christian women get a bad rap in my opinion. I'm not saying that it's right for our husbands to cheat, that their cheating is the cause of us living dysfunctionally, or that our joint dysfunction is an excuse for that behavior, but what

I am saying is that we have to take responsibility for the part we play and make the necessary changes so we can receive everything God has for us and our families according to His promises. Get the help you need so that you can be in a better place mentally, spiritually, physically and financially. Find a counselor, coach, or mentor to support you in your season of singleness and to support you when you're married.

Your life matters, and if it didn't, the enemy wouldn't be attacking you so hard. God has such a beautiful plan for your life and you cannot afford to stay bound with fear, unforgiveness, bitterness, or resentment. Letting go is really the key to the balancing act! When our hearts are free, our eyes are then opened to deeper levels and realms in the spirit, and this is where vision is birthed. Vision that will unlock your joy, happiness, peace, and prosperity. True balance starts with you, it's from the inside-out. I could never have loved my husband the way I do now if God did not allow those things to happen. Because He did allow those things, realignment and romance was reignited in my marriage.

Sierra Hilaire: Married 15 Years

As a single woman, whether you've been married before or never, taking care of yourself is vital to the health of any relationship you will get into while you are waiting on God. When I got married at the age of nineteen, I was so blind and unaware of what it really meant to be a Proverbs 31 woman or wife. Developing a healthy relationship with yourself by spending time getting to know you, defining your core values, your mission, and vision are all important parts of living a balanced life and managing your time. When your husband finds you, you will have already mastered the art of prioritization. Things will definitely be different, but you will have the skills to readjust as needed to stay committed to your vows. It's not about what your husband does or doesn't do, it's about you being faithful to who you are and what you stand for. Your husband will honor and admire that about you because you are confident in who you are in Christ and in self.

I'm so grateful to God that we went through that difficult time. Because of it, I am now equipped to share this story with you in hopes of you gaining insight and wisdom to avoid certain mistakes and pitfalls. I'm also hopeful that it will help you heal and recover if you've been through something like this and you're unsure of how you will handle another relationship. Forgiveness was the thing that set me free to relentlessly pursue my purpose. Although I got knocked out a few times, I stayed in the ring because I know that the fight is already fixed in my favor.

My prayer for you is that you would fall so in love with your Heavenly Father that self and spouse care would be second nature and you won't have to struggle to be happy or successful. I pray that God would heal your heart if it's hurting, and that he will send you a husband that will love you past your fears, insecurities, doubts, and even your past.

If you are in need of a coach to partner with you on this journey, as a Self-Care Strategist, my mission is to see women activated to be authentic, balanced, and free to relentlessly pursue their purpose! Connect with me on social media @SierraHilaire or visit my website www.SierraHilaire.com to contact me and to subscribe to my email list for inspiration, tips, and special offers.

Remember 1st Peter 5:8, *"Be well balanced and always alert, because your enemy, the devil, roams around incessantly, like a roaring lion looking for its prey to devour."*

May I

Poetess Ashali Snead

Black man,
My Man,
My future and man with the plan.
May I love on you??
Like this?
From the heart, from deep in my soul?
Will you settle a moment and let me have control?
One night is all I ask.
This is my pleasure, not a task.
Your feet have traveled MANY miles,
Your shoulders carry much weight.
Your brain runs nonstop, figuring out your next
move to make.
You're a father, son, uncle, cousin, friend and
brother,
Yet, to me, you're my lover!
Many hats you wear,
tonight tho,
I need to uncover and unlock
The other parts you don't see.
As I rub you down,

Sit back, close your eyes,
And... just... Breathe!
Ecstasy exists, and I'm gonna take you there.
The mood is set, now open your eyes and stare...
Into... me... see,
relax,
deep breaths,
and feel my energy,
For it is a gift that you well deserve.
You are more than enough if you haven't heard.
So I ask you again,
May I love on you??
Like this?
From the heart, from deep in my soul?
Will you settle a moment and relinquish your
control?
Do you trust me enough?
If so, relax and LET GO.

About the Co-Authors

 **Regine Joseph** is an innovative prophetic voice and visionary called to curate Kingdom experiences for life, love, and leisure. She is the CEO of Regine Joseph Enterprises which houses her signature coaching program, Not a Broken Vessel, an event planning firm, A Royal Affair, and an inspirational apparel line, Royal-T shirts. Regine is also Co-Founder of 2 Chix with a Camera Photography Company, where her mission is to capture the glory in the stories of her clients. She also enjoys spending time with her four children, Dashna, Sabrina, Elizabeth, and Olumide and takes pride in keeping them fully engaged in her business ventures to pass the entrepreneurial mantle on to their generation.

Tonika Goode is a coach, consultant, author, and minister of the Word of God. She is currently working on her master's in education with an anticipated completion date of May 2021. Tonika's gift is to assist people from all walks of life by helping them to see the diamond in themselves.

Audrey Brooks is a Board-Certified Christian Counselor and Master Life Coach. She empowers individuals to release the past, resist stagnation, and arise from spiritually desolate places by igniting passion to purpose and provoking forward progress by generating growth. Audrey's desire is her work, which helps individuals redirect their mind, restore their heart, and recreate purpose. She is a wife of 34 years and the mother of three children.

Berlinda Grant is a Registered Nurse, Wellness Strategist, and CEO of Perfect Imperfections. "My is mission to empower women to embrace their Perfect Imperfections through self-awareness, customized coaching, and engaging events that promote optimal wellness to maximize their potential, possibilities, and purpose. I am grateful for the times I get to spend with my kids, with my grandson, and in exploring different cuisine.

Mia Roan is a woman of God who has been married for more than half of her years on earth. She desires to know the heart of the heavenly Father, whom she did not make her first husband, first. Mia is committed to the discovery of the *predestined me* and to the walking out of her life.

About the Co-Authors

Ebony Nicole Smith is the writing coach and publisher to entrepreneurs and clergy who desire to create books that can become an additional stream of income. She is the founder and CEO of Ebony Nicole Smith Consulting, LLC, a boutique writing and publishing company based in Rochester, New York. Ebony is a 2015 ROC Awards nominee for Author of the Year and Mayoral Recognition for Small MWBE (Minority Women-owned Business Enterprise) in Rochester NY 2020. She has written and published 10 books of her own and 20 for her clients. An author by passion, transformational speaker by experience, and a woman of God by calling, Ebony Nicole wears many hats. In addition to running her business, she is the co-founder of and the chairwoman for the Rochester Black Authors Association, radio co-host of The Inspirational Experience: Cornerstone Wednesdays on 100.9 WXIR FM, and the Guest Services Director of the Rochester Black Men Achieve Awards. She lives in Rochester NY with her family and travels the world with her heart.

Chenique Pinder is an Author, Inspirational Speaker, Certified Family Empowerment Coach, and CEO of Feet to Faith Family Services, Inc., a non-profit organization that serves at risk youth and their families. Mrs. Pinder has accepted the mission to equip and empower men and women with the skills and tools needed to establish their families on a foundation of faith. Chenique wants to see holistic restoration in families and has made a clarion call in communities to influence culture and affect change for the glory of God. Turning her brokenness and pain into passion and purpose, she holds firmly to Romans 8:28, emphasizing "ALL things!"

T. Lewis-English is a Licensed Practitioner Nurse, CEO and Founder of Grace of Hannah an Infertility Support Organization, Author, and Advocate for infertility issues.

Debra Pope Reddick is the visionary leader of Debra Reddick Ministries. She is a Co- Pastor, teacher, intercessor, Author, speaker, conference planner, and facilitator, and a certified life coach. She has a mandate to equip the saints of God so that they may fulfill their unique purpose in life. She utilizes her spiritual gifts, as the Holy Spirit leads, to direct, instruct, and strengthen women in their walk with Jesus Christ. Pastor Debra operates in a yoke-destroying anointing, which was birthed through various adversities in her own life. Pastor Debra is a two-time survivor of Breast Cancer. She feels that God has given her one of her greatest assignments: to be able to stand beside her husband, Pastor Terance C. Reddick as Co-Pastor.

 **A. B. Brumfield** is the founder and CEO of two publishing companies, through which she has been a publisher for over ten years. She is the founder, CEO, and chief editor of her editing firm with over thirteen years of professional editing experience. She is an author with nine published books and two published short stories in her literary repertoire. With being a "living reflection of God" as her first order of business, A.B. spends her days doing the work God has called her to do, which encompasses spreading the gospel of Jesus Christ through her God given, spiritual gifts of writing, speaking, and teaching to all God makes available to her.

Diana L. Morrow is a Minister, Master Spiritual Coach, and Professional Conference Speaker. She is the founder of One Global Voice In Christ Ministries, a ministry dedicated to teaching and training women all over the world how to become true worshippers and intercessors for Christ so that they can receive the manifestations of the promises of God. Diana currently lives in the Rochester NY area with her husband Vern and they are the proud parents of nine adult children, and many grandchildren while enjoying their empty nest.

Felicia Barnett: Pastor Felicia has an MBA degree from Everest University. Over many years of serving in ministry, Pastor Felicia developed Christian education programs, outreach programs, facilitated many services, and has delivered God's message to many souls. Her mission and vision is to empower women to overcome life adversities through advocacy, accountability, and community based programs that build faith and birth purpose: Women reconciled, restored and resilient.

 **M. Denise Simmons** is an Award-Winning, Haitian-American Producer, Director, and Miami Native. M. Denise Simmons creates provocative films that explore humanity, race relations, urban crime, and violence. Her film "#BeforeYouShoot", which aims to humanize the lives of black men in America in the eyes of law enforcement, media, and society is the 2019 Urban Film Festival Winner for Best Documentary Feature Film. The film has birthed the non-profit organization, #BeforeYouShoot Foundation, Inc. which empowers youth and young adults to identify various issues in their communities such as poverty, gang/gun violence, and education while also providing them the tools to create content that both raise awareness and help to resolve these issues. Denise is a graduate of the University of Florida with a Bachelor of Science in Public Relations and a Minor in Business Administration. She is the loving wife of Deacon Mario Simmons and they are the proud parents of two handsome boys, Christian and Solomon.

Maryann Rivera-Dannert is The Fearless Living Coach and a Human Resources Professional. A Certified Life Coach, her life's mission is to empower, inspire, and equip women from coast to coast to gain self-confidence as they create the life they've always desired, a life where they are free and happy, living life on their terms, through one on one or group coaching. Maryann also has a YouTube channel where she shares her message of fearlessness and fabulousness. Overcoming adversity, she has turned her life around and the once high school dropout, is now a four-time published best-selling author, holds a Master's degree in Leadership and a Bachelor's degree in Organizational Management. Maryann currently resides in the state of Florida and she enjoys the beach, traveling, and spending time with her family.

Regine McNish, faithful servant to the Lord Jesus Christ and wife to her wonderful husband, Regina is the President and Creative Director for a community based praise dance ministry, "We Fight to Tell Stories" (WFTTS). She was born and raised in Ft. Lauderdale Fl. From an early age she knew her life was different. She would always find a secluded spot to write, sing, or dance. Her passion for Christ has allowed her to evolve and in the midst of it all, to seek God. All of her life, she knew that she would be an author, she just did not have a clue it would be today. Born in the middle of seven siblings, Regine found that it was not an easy road to find her purpose. With a mother who had a third-grade education and a father who never loved her, she would embark on the long journey called life. Despite all the odds that were stacked against her, she was able to prevail only by the grace of God. Today is a new day for Regina because she is set free from her past and able to move forward with Christ leading the way.

Sierra Hilaire is a Certified Self-Care Strategist, Pastor, Author, and the CEO/Founder of Sierra Hilaire Enterprise and Divine Potential Services, Inc. Her ultimate passion and purpose in life is to see women activated to be authentic, balanced, and free to relentlessly pursue their purpose by teaching them how to manage stress, to simplify life, and to become self-sufficient by building a faith-based business. She loves great food, books, and spending time with her husband, children, and community.

Veigh Floyd is a Youth Pastor, Entrepreneur, and Human Resource Professional in Upstate New York. She is also a women's mentor and counselor whose desire is to help guide women from all walks of life around and through life's puddles, potholes, and pitfalls, and to teach them to make mentally, emotionally, and psychologically healthy choices. Her greatest desire is to present a woman with a balanced perspective to whatever issue she may be facing, to see her win, succeed, see herself as God sees her, and ultimately to love herself! Veigh holds a Bachelor's degree in Organizational Management, and a certificate in Interior Design. She loves to travel with her husband and daughter on family vacations.

 **Wynsome S. McLean** is an author, Licensed Marriage and Family Therapist in the State of Florida, and Owner of Soul Care Institute, LLC. She has a Bachelor's degree in Psychology from Georgia State University, and a Master's degree in Marriage and Family Therapy. Wynsome is an ordained Revered in the Church of God of Cleveland Tennessee and faithfully serves as Co-Pastor of Bread of Life International Church of God alongside her husband Bishop Harvey McLean. She is the Pastor of Care and Counseling and a Certified Vision Strategist with Impart Kingdom Ministries. Wynsome is passionate about seeing a total transformation of the soul and realizing God's vision for all mankind.

About the Poets

 **Kalina Harrison** is an Atlanta native who currently lives in the City of Brotherly Love. As the CEO of Kreative Scribes, Kalina writes personal development books, creates marketing content for professional brands, and facilitates entrepreneurship-based workshops to teach the youth how to start a business. "Written Visions Coming to Fruition" and "Motivation to Activation: A 12-Step Guide to Activating Your Success" are her latest self-published books.

 **Ashali Snead** is your favorite stylist, educator, and motivator. As a licensed stylist and the proud owner of The Loc Lounge in Rochester NY, Ashali's vision for the future is to expand her positive energy, to motivate, and to heal others through motivational speaking and music which she started with her first and sold out show, "Locs and Love Songs". Her voice can be heard on her recently released Podcast "Ash (Ask) Me Anything" on all outlets. Ashali believes the message for every aspect of life is simple, a Godly life is a balanced life. Do what you have to do to find and keep it for each season.

Raquel K. Walker sweetly embraces life and uses her experiences to fuel her journey to self-actualization. A lover of the arts and women's and youth empowerment, Raquel uses her passion to mentor, coach, guide, and teach those with whom she comes in contact. Her love of writing and the benefits of sharing deeply with others has drawn her to the opportunity to support the 6th season production of *Listen to Your Mother*. Her quest is to continue to creatively support members of our organizations, members of our families, and members of our communities. We often wade through, and have sometimes sat too long, with who we are not before getting to who we are. There we find our connection to the whole. Raquel Walker strides forward filled with a healthy dose of fear and a perpetual feeling of courage. She is a business owner and visionary, a licensed massage therapist, a mother, a wife, a teacher, and a lifelong student.

About the Poets

August Love loves spending time with friends one on one or small groups yet jumps at the opportunity to deliver a presentation or give a speech. She is socially selective but loves to network. She has zero tolerance for cliques, ass kissing, and phony people.

She is a creative and innovate leader who occasionally reads her poems at open mic night. She volunteers her time to create platforms for Black people. She is committed to black empowerment, black pride, black excellence and black progress.

August's hobbies include traveling, patronizing and promoting Black businesses. She loves ice wine, going to the beach, and empowering others.

Reflections

Reflect to Grow, To Renew, To Become a Successfully
Single Woman and Future Successful Wife

Made in the USA
Columbia, SC
12 September 2020

20588434R00134